Welcome

For centuries Buddhist thinkers have believed there is a connection between mind and body, emotional well-being and physical health. Yet despite more and more people turning to mindfulness and meditation to help them stay afloat in today's hectic modern world, scientists seem unable to agree on what mindfulness actually does, or even what it is. So can this ancient practice really help those of us struggling to meet the often conflicting demands of home, work, family, and friends?

Evidence is growing that mindfulness can act as a buffer against these stresses. So much today can seem fast and frenzied, feel transitory, and of an impersonal nature. Mindfulness gives you the chance to slow things down, to find some headspace to develop interests, strengthen relationships, and look after yourself. And with these can come new intentions: to be more mindful about how to begin and treasure each day, to be more grateful for all those little things that can make such a difference, to be more spontaneous and try something new.

We delve into all of this and more in this *Breathe Mindfulness Special*. Think of it as your chance to take a breath and explore more deeply what it is that makes you truly happy. Perhaps it will open up fresh ways of seeing the world and help you to realise you can make a difference, however small it may seem.

www.breathemagazine.co.uk

Contents

©2019 Guild of Master Craftsman Publications Ltd.

Design: Jo Chapman. **Editorial**: Susie Duff, Catherine Kielthy, Jane Roe. **Publisher**: Jonathan Grogan. **Cover illustration**: Trina Dalziel.
Produced by Guild of Master Craftsman Publications Ltd. 86 High Street, Lewes, BN7 1XN, United Kingdom.

The science of mindfulness

Based on ancient Buddhist practices, mindfulness has increasingly entered into the mainstream. But what does it actually mean and is there scientific evidence to convince the nonbelievers?

"Mindfulness" has become something of a buzzword when it comes to emotional and physical self-care. Increasingly, the practice is used to help with everything from mild anxiety to depression, with a growing body of research backing up the benefits to overall well-being.

However, with no clear scientific agreement about how mindfulness works—and even what it is—you might question whether it can really help those of us who are struggling to keep up with the frenetic pace of today's world. While it's true there is still much to be understood, several reliable studies have begun to unravel the science behind mindfulness. And while it's not a miracle cure for every psychological or physical problem, there's no doubt that it is a helpful practice for many people.

So, what is mindfulness?

The word has variously been used to describe a psychological state of awareness, the practices that promote such awareness, a way of processing information, and a character trait. With so many definitions, it's little wonder that the subject can start to feel like something of a minefield.

Perhaps the simplest way to think about mindfulness is as an "in-the-moment" awareness. It's about fully focusing on whatever it is that you're doing. Take a mundane task such as washing up, for example. Your mind will naturally want to wander, but simply noticing the warmth of the water on your skin and the way the bubbles float up, before—pop!—they're gone, can help you to be 100 percent present—and mindful.

Mindfulness versus meditation

Although the popularity of mindfulness has rocketed in recent years, the Western world has "borrowed" and adapted the practice from ancient Buddhist meditations. However, Dr. Judy Lovas, founder of Art & Science of Relaxation, a business which translates the science of mind-body health into everyday practice, is keen to highlight the difference between the two.

"Mindfulness is not the same as meditation [which uses a more disciplined form of concentration], since it can be applied to everyday activities like checking emails, preparing meals, and spending time with your family," explains Judy.

"Mindfulness can be defined as an awareness of what is currently happening around us, both internally and externally, without being judgmental."

To drill down still further, it's about learning to relate to your thoughts and feelings as mental "events" rather than things that are or aren't true. Think of them as clouds rolling through the sky. They are simply there and will pass. According to research, this increased observation and awareness of your daily thinking patterns can help you to disengage from repetitive and unhelpful ones. This, in turn, can give you better control over your emotions.

Mindfulness as therapy

Professionals in the field of psychology have certainly embraced its power. Over the past 25 years, therapists have developed specific mindfulness programs to help with conditions including anxiety, depression, and the

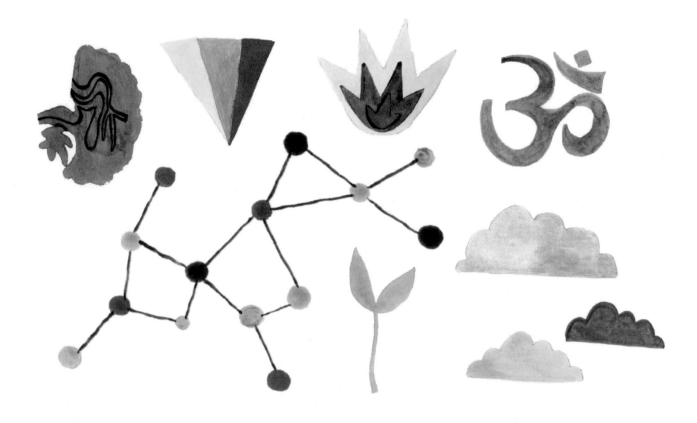

stress associated with dealing with long-term physical illness. Mindfulness-Based Stress Reduction (MBSR) is an eight-week program that teaches mindfulness skills in a group setting to use in daily life, while Mindfulness-Based Cognitive Therapy (MBCT) combines the structure of MBSR with cognitive behavioral therapy. Individuals who experience recurrent depression might find this approach useful in light of the finding that relapse can be associated with "negative" thinking patterns such as catastrophizing, self-criticism, and rumination. Mindfulness helps to challenge and shift away from those habitual thoughts.

And it seems that you don't have to sit in on the therapist's couch, either, to experience the benefits. Mindfulness can be pretty effective when learned online: a 2018 report in the journal *Mindfulness* evaluated the effect of the online MBCT "Be Mindful" course. People completing the course reported a 63 percent decrease in depression, 58 percent reduction in anxiety, and a 40 percent reduction in perceived stress. And this was no flash in the pan: the effects held steady at three- and six-month follow-ups.

The results are in

Research conducted by respected and trustworthy sources certainly demonstrates both the physical and psychological benefits. These include a decrease in symptoms of anxiety and depression, pain management,

plus a reduction in sleep disorders. A 2013 trial published in the *Journal of Clinical Psychiatry* found that people with generalized anxiety disorder who were treated with MBSR showed a significantly greater reduction in anxiety and distress ratings—and a greater increase in positive self-statements—when compared to those given stress-management advice.

Meanwhile, a 2014 study looking at recurring depression makes for striking and persuasive reading. Conducted by The Oxford Centre for Mindfulness in the UK, the year-long research found that MBCT reduced recurrent depressive episodes by 40 to 50 percent in comparison to other methods. And the *Journal of Consulting and Clinical Psychology* went one step further in a report the previous year, claiming that MBCT is as effective at reducing recurrence as antidepressant medications.

It's all in the mind

In fact, according to Boccia et al's *The Meditative Mind: A Comprehensive Meta-Analysis of MRI Studies*, a regular mindfulness practice may even cause emotions to be processed differently in the brain, enabling people to experience them more selectively. This chimes with the earlier point about learning to be aware of your thoughts and feelings. Honing these new self-observation skills helps to disengage automatic pathways in the nervous system that were created by previous learning, allowing current input to

be integrated in a fresh way. Researchers believe that brain changes like these lead to more flexible thinking.

Do you ever feel unreasonably upset when watching a sad movie? If you're getting through a box of tissues within the first five minutes, mindfulness could be the surprising solution. A 2010 experiment found that participants who had undertaken MBSR had less nervous system reactivity when they were shown sad movies than a control group, showing a strong link between the therapy and a reduction in emotional reactivity.

Research also indicates that the prefrontal lobe of the brain—a place your stress reactions come from—shrinks with regular mindfulness practice. As a result, you may be able to access "higher order" regions in the brain, leading to improved levels of self-insight, morality, intuition, and control of fear.

Other research explored the benefits of mindfulness in the management of long-term physical conditions. In a 2012 review of 114 studies, the use of mindfulness-based treatments for people with poor physical health was found to lead to improvements in mental well-being, reducing stress, anxiety, and depression.

A balanced view

Of course, there is a flipside to consider, says Buddhist Toni Bernhard, author of *How To Live Well With Chronic Pain And Illness*. In her column in *Psychology Today*, she notes that if you have unresolved psychological issues or trauma, mindfulness and meditation may not always be the best choice. She argues: "When your mind becomes quiet and calm, repressed or charged thoughts and emotional issues can come up—issues you may have been keeping at arm's length or that you didn't even realize existed.

"Mindfulness is an excellent tool for seeing that you need not believe in or act upon the ever-changing array of thoughts and emotions that arise in the mind. But if these thoughts and emotions are the result of deeply embedded psychological problems, they can stick in your mind and increase in intensity, leading to anxiety, anxiousness, and fearfulness."

It's important to remember that mindfulness isn't a panacea for your problems, nor a shortcut to a state of constant bliss, so be wary of outsized expectations. It does, however, offer clear benefits that are backed by science, making it, at the very least, a worthwhile addition to your wellness toolkit.

And as Dr. Judy Lovas explains, you don't need to devote huge chunks of time to mindfulness to reap the benefits. Starting out with being mindful for between two to five minutes every day can be beneficial: "Evidence highlights that it is the regularity of practice, not the duration, that improves well-being," she says.

"Being attentive to the task of the moment is mindfulness and repeating this regularly is the key to success."

WORDS: SOPHIA AULD. ILLUSTRATIONS: SARA THIELKER

Ways to start your day
with intention

How often have you read articles about how the most successful people leap out of bed at 5am to run a few miles, practice yoga, drink green smoothies, and get a head start on their to-do list? For some, that's the best way to start the day. But it doesn't work for everyone—we're not all morning people. And for many, a child's voice or a pet's paw on the face is the signal that the day has begun. Nonetheless, it is possible to bring more intention into the morning and set a positive tone. Giving a little attention to your mental approach as you go about your waking routine can change the trajectory of your whole day. Here are five ways you could begin your morning on a positive, nourishing note. Try one, some or all of them—whatever fits best with you and your schedule.

1 While your head is still on the pillow

You're awake, your day is beginning and your mind is starting to fill with all the things you need to do. You know you need to get going but before you heave yourself out of bed take a moment to practice a little loving-kindness. This ancient meditation extends kindness to yourself and to others, and while it seems very simple it can really improve how you feel at the start of the day.

First, picture yourself as you are, lying in bed. Then repeat these sentences to yourself a couple of times:

May I be safe
May I be happy
May I be healthy
May I live with ease

If your attention is so in demand from your family that you can't spend a moment more in bed then at least say these words to yourself. By being self-compassionate, you will be in a better position to give to others.

If you can manage to stay between the sheets for a few more minutes, extend the loving-kindness outward to others. Imagine someone you love and repeat the sentences again, replacing "I" with "he" or "she." Finally, hold a wider group of people in your mind, perhaps your colleagues, neighbors, or friends, and repeat the words again, replacing "I" with "they."

This is a shortened, simplified version of loving-kindness meditation but it gets across the basic points of extending compassion to yourself and others. Taking a moment to say these words will give your day a more positive intention than simply rolling out of bed with a groan.

2 While in the bathroom

Choose one of your daily rituals such as brushing your teeth, washing your hair, or moisturizing your face, and make it a mindful activity. For this brief time put aside everything you have to tackle over the course of the day and focus your attention on what you're doing in this moment. Feel the tube in your hand as you squeeze toothpaste onto your brush, watch how your mouth changes shape as you move the toothbrush around, notice how the toothpaste tastes and smells. You don't need to have an opinion on what you're doing, or judge your brushing technique—this is simply about noticing what's taking place at this moment, just as it is. Your to-do list will still be there when you finish in the bathroom, there's no need to mentally bring it in with you, into this time.

3 While you get dressed

You could turn this into another mindful activity, focusing on the action of putting on clothes, or you could use this time to practice another positive intention—gratitude. Think of something, or several things, that you're thankful for right now. The more specific the better and it can be as small as you like. There's no need to hunt for something momentous. You could be thankful your child slept until past 6am; that you feel prepared for today's meeting; that the sun is shining; or that your outfit doesn't need ironing. Think about why you're thankful and let yourself soak in the gratitude. It's easy to leap forward into imagining the day ahead, which could cause you to worry and feel apprehensive. This short gratitude practice reminds you of what is already good.

4 While you're getting ready

It may feel like your morning has begun at a breakneck speed but you still have the rest of the day stretching ahead of you. What do you want to do today? What would feel like an achievement? What would simply be enough? It doesn't need to be a big goal or a triumph at work. It might be to take a 20-minute lunch break or to clean the bathroom or even to be kind to yourself. What is one thing you could do today that would feel like success, however small, and in whatever shape? Create that one intention for yourself.

5 Before you get down to any work

Following on from creating a specific intention for the day, take a moment to consider how you want to feel and create an affirmation or mantra to use as a reminder over the next few hours. For example, if you're feeling nervous, you could give yourself the affirmation "I am brave" or "I am strong." If you want to feel energized, it might be "I am ready for today" or "I can do this." If today will involve asserting your opinion or authority, "I am in charge of my life" or "I believe in me" may help.

Creating a mantra can be a useful tool to remind yourself of how you want to feel or behave. If today is a day you want to savor and bank in your memory, "be here now" can remind you to stay in the present moment. Think of a message that you would love a friend to say to you today, something that would help you right now, and say it yourself. Note it down on a piece of paper or in your phone so you can reference and repeat it throughout the day.

There are many ways to begin each day with mindful intention—these are just a few relatively easy ones to get you started. Everyone has a morning routine, schedule, and time constraints to work within so try out different ideas and see which ones work best for you.

BEAUTY IN THE EVERYDAY

Rather than seeing mindfulness as a complicated, time-consuming task to add to the to-do list, try to find time for reflection in your daily routine

The benefits of mindfulness are plentiful, yet sometimes the advice on how to live a more reflective life in a busy world can seem contradictory, with gurus offering enlightenment through complex and lengthy routines and exercises. The fortunate truth is that you can reach a state of gentle meditation without the need for prolonged spells of sitting still while the daily to-do list screams for your attention. Those must-do chores won't go away, so why not combine them with a healthy dose of mindfulness and experience the best of both worlds?

Teacher, consultant, and therapist Kathryn Lovewell is a passionate believer in the benefits of approaching routine activities with thoughtful love and attention. She delivers a training program in Mindful Self-Compassion, where participants are encouraged to practice mindfulness in their daily lives—essentially looking at everyday tasks in a new and different light. "Things like making your afternoon cup of coffee or taking a hot morning shower are just perfect," she says.

It sounds easy enough, but where do you start? During the course Kathryn invites participants to get in the zone by choosing an activity they do every day. "Pick something you would usually do without thinking," she says. "Bring it to mind and visualize yourself doing it. Fully immerse yourself in it, pay attention to your senses and really savor the experience." This could be anything from eating your lunch to sitting on the bus—nothing is too mundane.

There are many benefits—physical, mental, and emotional—to be had by practicing this method. In just a few minutes the mind becomes calmer, stress hormones are reduced, and the body relaxes. By focusing on the here and now you move away from ruminating thoughts of situations that may be getting you down or causing you anxiety. This in turn helps to distance yourself from any unpleasant emotions that these situations may be causing. And by embedding this fresh approach in your normal day-to-day routine you establish a new healthy habit that also brings the benefits of mindfulness.

NOW IT'S YOUR TURN

Start by choosing an everyday activity. Keep it simple. It could be brushing your teeth, preparing breakfast, or, like Ruth, washing up after a meal. Here we're using the example of hanging out the laundry...

- *Breathe*—before you get started, take three deep breaths: in through the nose, filling the lungs with air and pushing out the belly, before slowly exhaling through the mouth as though you are gently blowing out a candle.
- *Feel*—notice the shapes your arms make as you take each garment out of the laundry basket and hang it on the line. Do you keep your back straight or slightly bent as you lift?

- *Observe*—watch how shirts, T-shirts, and even socks move with the wind. Now look around you. What else is happening in your yard? Are there leaves on the ground, clouds in the sky? Can you see any birds or wildlife moving in the undergrowth or up in the trees? Is it cold or warm?
- *Smell*—can you make out the fragrance of your cleaner or fabric conditioner? And what other scents are competing with it?

- *Taste*—is there dew in the air that's fallen onto your lips? What sensation does it bring?
- *Listen*—what sounds can you hear? The whoosh of freshly laundered sheets taken up by the breeze? Is there traffic noise in the background? Tune in to what's around you.
- *Breathe*—finish with three long, slow, deep breaths, as before. Close your eyes for a moment. Pause to check how you feel before continuing with the rest of your day.

Ruth Atkinson, a bank employee and a mother, has taken the mindful approach to washing up: "I've always been quite particular about washing the dishes," she says. "I like to do it 'properly,' but have recently found it particularly therapeutic. I start with putting on my rubber gloves and like to soak up the fragrance of the washing-up liquid while swirling the water. I'm quite methodical, washing items in a particular order and working through from cutlery up to pans, lining everything up as I go. It feels so satisfying and soothing.

"Even if the family are in the kitchen it's something I like to do in silence. It's become a ritual and I always finish by burning some incense. It's as though I'm 'putting the kitchen to bed' after the evening meal," she says. "The kitchen window looks out onto the garden, which my dad takes great pride in keeping beautiful, and I pause regularly to take a good look at it. I love noticing the changes from day to day—it rained heavily one day last week and the flowers seemed more vibrant afterward. It's nice to chat to my dad later about what I've noticed. He seems to appreciate this and that's a lovely bonding experience between us in itself."

A soothing ritual, the beauty of nature, precious bonding time, and a chore ticked off. Almost makes you want to reach for the rubber gloves, doesn't it?

Follow this mindful approach to any of life's routine tasks and in time you may notice yourself feeling calmer and less stressed.

WORDS: SIMONE SCOTT. ILLUSTRATIONS: LOU BAKER SMITH

Go slow and get ahead

Rushing through a never-ending to-do list, multitasking, working through your lunch hour. In today's hectic world it can feel as if everyone is obsessed with getting more done. Yet there's evidence that slowing down at work can improve productivity—and happiness

Time. It's one of the great challenges of modern working life. People make lists, prioritize, and restructure their days: all with the aim of finding more time, to do more, to be more. Despite all of these efforts, weekends are often spent recovering, while desperately trying to achieve some semblance of a healthy work/life balance.

Ask most people and they will tell you that they are working more. Indeed, according to a 2018 Work and Well-being Survey conducted by the American Psychological Association, 42 percent of employees say they struggle with too heavy a workload, while 39 percent cited long hours as an issue. Add to this the push to work smarter—technology has made people available 24/7—and it's little wonder absenteeism is on the increase.

A recent World Health Organization-led study estimates that depression and anxiety disorders cost the global economy US$1 trillion each year in lost productivity. With many people destined to spend a quarter of their adult life at work, balancing it with personal and family time is an ongoing priority. At home many people are slowing down while at work, they're running at maximum speed.

The case for slow

Author Carl Honoré first described this cultural backlash against the hyperactivity of modern life in his 2005 book *In Praise of Slow: How a Worldwide Movement is Challenging the Cult of Speed*. Reflecting on the increasing number of people choosing to slow down, he wrote: "In every human endeavor you can think of, from sex,

work, and exercise to food, medicine, and urban design, these rebels are doing the unthinkable—they are making room for slowness. And the good news is that decelerating works."

Because, like Aesop's fable of the tortoise and the hare, slowing down can achieve surprising results. By decelerating, there's suddenly time to reflect on priorities, brainstorm problems, and come up with new ideas, focus on happiness, and make changes to rebalance.

As Vanessa King, lead positive psychology expert for Action for Happiness and author of *The Ten Keys to Happier Living*, points out: "Work plays a big role in people's lives. It impacts how well they parent, how well they look out for their neighbors, and how much energy and passion they put into other areas of interest beyond work." There is a growing body of research by medical practitioners and psychologists that supports the case for slow working. According to Professor Mika Kivimäki et al, not only is overwork and related stress a factor in increased likelihood of stroke and heart disease, but working longer hours also does not increase the ability to get more done.

While the immediate response to escalating to-do lists is often to work longer and faster, studies suggest otherwise. Levin Professor of Economics John Pencavel of Stanford University has shown that productivity of an employee significantly declines after a 50-hour week and even more so after 55. Moreover, output at 70 hours of work differs little from that at 56, indicating the additional 14 hours achieved minimal achievement.

As for multitasking, a University of California report, *The Cost of Interrupted Work: More Speed and Stress*, suggests that when you jump from one task to another, it can take 25 minutes to refocus on what you were doing beforehand. Increased creativity and problem-solving are also improved by slowing down during the work day. Organizational psychologist Adam Grant advocates a healthy dose of procrastination. In his TED talk on this subject: "Procrastination gives you time to consider divergent ideas, to think in nonlinear ways, to make unexpected leaps."

You can even slow down your perception of time when you focus on the here and now according to neuroscientist David Eagleman. By opening yourself up to new things, your experience of time changes. This, he says, is because time and memory are deeply intertwined. When you try something new, your brain is more focused and it writes down more memories. So when you recall the incident, it appears to have taken longer.

Happiness at work

Happiness has become the yardstick for businesses and employee work satisfaction and well-being. How engaged people are, and how well they are able to perform their roles, are indicators of not only how happy they are at work, but also an organization's financial performance.

In his study of the 100 Best Companies to Work For in America, Professor Alex Edmans of the London Business School in the UK found that over a 26-year period companies that invested in their people consistently outperformed their peers. When it comes to happiness at work, everyone is responsible. "We need to think about what happiness means in its fullest sense, recognizing that it is a shared responsibility. Organizations can do

a lot to create the conditions but individuals also have to think about how to maintain their own well-being," says Vanessa.

Such empowerment is thought-provoking—it encourages you to assess entrenched habits in order to make significant changes to how you work. Slowing down can also help pinpoint individual successes, to identify when boundaries have been crossed, and to realign work priorities with personal values.

Importantly, small things can make the most difference. Vanessa recommends that you focus on work relationships in what she calls "short, positive interactions." These can be as simple as stopping and talking to a colleague, seeing beyond the task at hand, to expressing an interest in the person beyond their role. It's a small investment for what she describes as significant returns. She says when you are happy at work "you are literally more open to other people. You are more open to information and ideas. You are more flexible in your thinking and better at creative problem solving. You see more options."

Critically, the ability to make connections and have meaningful conversations is dependent on time. In *Happy at Work Manifesto*, author Alexander Kjerulf writes: "I will take time to do this. Making myself and others happy at work takes time. Time is well spent because being happy makes me more productive."

Only by slowing down, by giving yourself the time to invest in yourself and others, do you start to achieve real happiness. Paradoxical as it may seem, by decelerating, you can gain more time. In doing so, you may discover that work satisfaction, creativity, and productivity don't come from working faster or even smarter, but by going slower.

HOW TO SLOW DOWN AT WORK

Mindfulness
With it taking 25 minutes to refocus once you are distracted, concentrating on one task at a time can slow you down. It's not as easy as it sounds because the way you work is rooted in habit, so nominate a single task each day to focus on and work from there.

Tilting
Rather than pursuing the ideal of a work/life balance, Brooke McAlary in her book *Destination Simple: Everyday Rituals for a Slower Life*, advocates tilting. "Instead of exhausting yourself by trying to achieve balance, learn to tilt. To willingly throw things out of balance. It's about understanding and accepting the fact that you cannot and will not ever achieve perfect balance." So begin by writing down everything that is most important, from family and friends to me-time and work. Then tilt within this sphere, knowing that you cannot be all things to all people.

Daily rituals
In the same way that people create rituals in their daily lives that provide enjoyment and pleasure, simple rituals at work can have a similar effect. Drinking tea from a beautiful cup or eating lunch from a handcrafted bowl offer opportunities to enjoy the beauty of the moment.

Take a break
Evidence shows that a short break, meditation, and even a walk in the park can increase performance. A 2017 survey by the National Charity Partnership reported that only 30 percent of those surveyed took a proper lunch break even though nine in 10 revealed going outside made them feel happier or more positive. So give yourself a 15-minute break and see what difference it makes.

Greening the office
Take inspiration from The Good Life Project based in Cambridgeshire, UK, which is researching the cognitive and emotional impact of a greater interaction with nature at work and in education. Doing something as simple as keeping a plant on your desk (or if you hot desk, a picture of your favorite green spot) can literally brighten your day.

Tuning out
At the heart of technology is the demand for presenteeism. Checking your emails on waking up and on the weekend robs you of downtime. Take the challenge of scheduling time to check-in, resisting the urge to be on-call.

Decluttering
In its 2011 Workspace Organization Survey, OfficeMax reported that U.S. executives waste six weeks a year searching for lost items and information. Clearing a desk can liberate you from this tyranny, both physically and metaphorically, giving you a clear space in which to think more freely and focus.

STAND UP FOR WHAT'S IMPORTANT

Making a distinction between what's urgent and what's important is harder than it sounds, but mastering the art could make you more efficient, more successful, and even more fulfilled

In 1954, a year after he was elected President, Dwight Eisenhower gave a speech at the Second Assembly of the World Council of Churches in Illinois, during which he read out a quote from a former college president. "I have two kinds of problems, the urgent and the important," he stated. "The urgent are not important, and the important are never urgent."

At first it seems like a nonsensical thing to say, but it actually makes a lot of sense. Over the years the idea of recognizing that what is urgent and what is important are often two different things has been adopted by politicians, business leaders, educators, and time-management consultants—rather fittingly, it's called the Eisenhower Principle.

Most people spend their time in firefighting mode, tackling urgent problems, leaving them no time for important tasks. Let's say, for example, you are at work when a colleague emails you to ask for your advice. You were planning a lunchtime run, but quickly abandon the idea to bail her out. While it might be the honorable thing to do, if it becomes a habit it could have a negative impact on your health—you have placed the urgent before the important.

This tendency to favor urgent tasks over important ones is understandable. Modern life is full of deadlines and time-specific tasks, making it easier to push actions that could help you to achieve your major life goals to the end of your to-do list. Some days it can feel as though you are bombarded by texts, emails, phone calls, and other interruptions, all claiming to be urgent, so it's easy to believe that these tasks are also important. Naturally, some of them will be, but more often than not they won't.

Humans are hotwired to react to urgent tasks and, as usual, we can blame our ancestors for this predisposition. Prehistoric man was frequently forced to think short-term to ensure his survival: If a saber-toothed tiger is heading your way it's obviously better to deal with the problem immediately rather than wait until it's within striking distance. A problem like this is both urgent and important. While the saber-toothed tiger has gone, however, the feeling that urgent always means important lingers on.

On the surface it might seem that by prioritizing urgent tasks you get more done. There's no denying that ticking little "urgent" jobs off your list is accompanied by a sense of satisfaction, but spending all your time completing tasks of low importance is counterproductive. You might take great pride in processing your inbox to empty every day, but if it leaves you unable to tackle tasks that could help you to achieve your life goals then you are, quite literally, wasting your time.

A fresh way of thinking

Thankfully, there is a solution, and it has the Eisenhower Principle at its core. In 1989 educator, businessman, and author Stephen Covey wrote *The 7 Habits of Highly Effective People*, a paperback that has since sold more than 25 million copies. The main takeaway is his diagram of the Time Management Matrix. This matrix (see overleaf) is essentially a square divided into quarters or "quadrants." The quadrants are labeled as follows: Quadrant 1: Important and urgent, Quadrant 2: Important, but not urgent, Quadrant 3: Not important, but urgent, and Quadrant 4: Not important, not urgent. It was Stephen's belief that every task you face can be assigned to one of these four quadrants. Before you assign a task to a quadrant you need to assess its genuine level of importance, and its genuine level of urgency. This can be tricky at times, so we're here to help—overleaf we look at each of the quadrants in turn and leave room for you to complete your own matrix.

Modern life is full of deadlines, making it easier to push actions that could help you achieve your major life goals aside

For a task to belong in Quadrant 1 (*important and urgent*) it needs to require immediate action, it should be screaming at you to do something. Stephen describes such tasks as "crisis, pressing problems, or deadline-driven projects." Examples include filing a tax return on deadline day, falling over and breaking your arm, or preparing for a meeting just hours before it starts. When something is urgent and important you need to act quickly, and often without much thought. There is no time to mull over the problem or weigh up the options. You are in crisis mode, and you are forced to react.

Most people will have a few tasks in Quadrant 1, but if you have more than that you need to reassess your priorities. "Quadrant 1 consumes many people," says Stephen. "They are crisis managers, problem-minded people, deadline-driven producers." What's more, tasks in this quadrant are unlikely to help you to achieve your life goals. In fact, they're more likely to tire you, sap energy, and leave you unable to tackle important jobs—those that support your core values or drive you forward. In an ideal world, Quadrant 1 will be almost empty.

Tasks that belong in Quadrant 2 (*important, but not urgent*) are a different beast entirely. This is the place for actions and activities that will assist you in achieving your personal and professional goals. Topics might include developing (or nurturing) relationships, long-term planning, prevention, and activities that support your core values. Examples might include spending more time with your partner, making plans to move house or change careers, or taking exercise to prevent illness. When you tackle tasks from this quadrant you are more likely to feel fulfilled and content, which is why Stephen suggests that Quadrant 2 should be your main focus. When something is important, but not urgent, you can respond to what is happening, rather than simply reacting.

Tasks that fall into Quadrant 3 (not important, but urgent) are often generated by other people and come in the form of interruptions (calls, emails, colleagues dropping by your desk, meetings). They rarely help you to reach your long-term goals, but they may help others reach theirs—only you can decide which is more important. Stephen suggests that many people spend most of their time completing tasks from this quadrant, while believing they are completing tasks from Quadrant 1 (important and urgent). It's an easy mistake to make— tasks in Quadrant 3 often involve helping other people, so they can feel important. What's more, they're often quick to finish, so you're rewarded with a shot of satisfaction. If you spend too much time pleasing other people or looking for that hit of satisfaction, however, you'll have no time left to pursue your life goals.

Quadrant 4 (*not important, not urgent*) is the home of distractions. Examples include social media, TV, spam in your inbox, and cold callers. Unless your life goal involves harnessing the power of social media or becoming a TV critic then these activities are a waste of time. But that's not to say you should avoid them altogether. After a hard day at work sometimes it can feel good to sit down in front of the TV or scroll through your newsfeed on Facebook. The trick is to do this mindfully, so with intention and full awareness. "Effective people stay out of Quadrants III and IV because, urgent or not, they aren't important," confirms Stephen.

At first glance the Eisenhower Principle (and the Time Management Matrix) might seem like time-management tools, but they are so much more than this. Their real purpose is to make you uncover where your true passions lie and then help you to make these passions your top priority. "The key is not to prioritize what's on your schedule, but to schedule your priorities," says Stephen. In short, you've got to stand up for what's important.

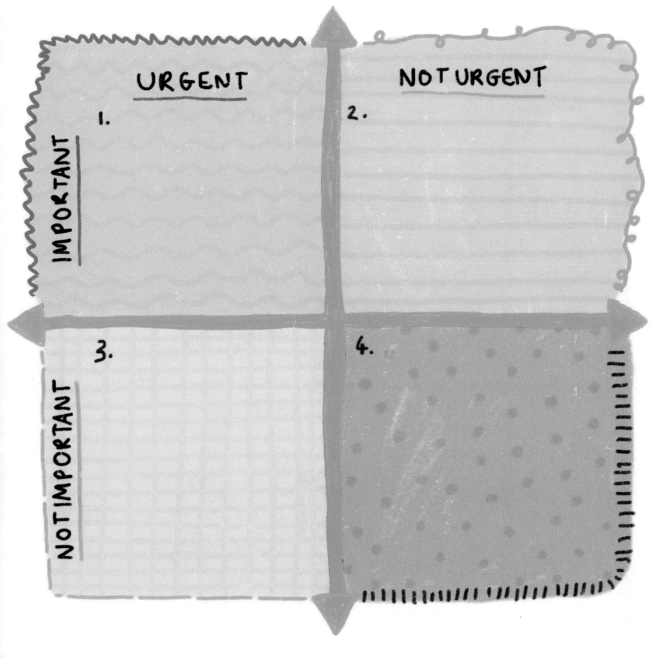

URGENT

NOT URGENT

1.

2.

IMPORTANT

3.

4.

NOT IMPORTANT

DECIDING BETWEEN WHAT'S IMPORTANT AND WHAT'S URGENT

Make a list of all of the tasks and activities you would like to complete in the next seven days. Place each item into one of the four quadrants in Stephen Covey's Time Management Matrix (above). Use the questions below to help you decide between what's important and what's urgent.

- Does the task help you to move forward with your long-term life or work goals?
- Has the task been generated by somebody else? If so, are you taking it on simply to placate them, or does it add value to your life?
- What will happen in a day/week/month/year if you do not complete a particular task?
- Is there somebody you could delegate the task to—failing that can you batch process tasks so you can carry out similar jobs (such as checking emails) in one session?

- What steps can you take to clear your schedule, and make room for tasks in Quadrant 2?
- Can you resist the urge to tackle an unimportant job just because it's quick to complete?
- Are you aware of how much time you spend indulging in the distractions listed in Quadrant 4? If not, use an app or jot down how many minutes you spend on these each day.
- Does a task in Quadrant 2 seem too big to complete? If so can you break it into smaller steps?

Smart move

*If your cell phone's determining how much time
you and it spend together, you need to take charge*

When was the last time you checked your phone to see
if you had a text, to scroll through Facebook posts, or
to have a quick look at a weather app? A few hours ago?
Within the last 30 minutes? Just this instant? According
to Apple, the average person unlocks their iPhone a
startling 80 times a day. That's approximately five times
an hour or every 12 minutes.

Test yourself. If you hear a beep, chime, or ding coming
from your phone, are you compelled to go and check it,
even if the odds suggest it's a promotional email sent by a
store you ordered from three years ago? Maybe you'll even
admit to unlocking your cell without receiving any alert,
just in case notifications have, for some bizarre reason,
stopped working.

There's no denying smartphones have their place
in today's technology-filled world. They're like a 21st-
century version of the Swiss Army knife, with an array of
efficient tools enabling you to communicate with others,
keep up to date with news, book vacations, monitor your
fitness levels, and so much more. But if dinnertime always
involves a phone sitting next to the salt and pepper, a cell
goes with you on every quick trip to the store, and hours
in the day seem mindlessly to disappear, then maybe the
digital life has gone too far.

In a recent study published by Deloitte UK, which
looked at whether smartphones are a blessing or a curse,
38 percent of respondents perceive they are using their
phone too much. They've become an essential everyday
item for individuals worldwide—the United Nations
claims there are more people around the world with
cell phones than have access to a flush toilet—but
is your phone dominating your life and beginning to
take control? Do you struggle when you're apart? If
you think your relationship is becoming unhealthy,
do something about it now.

Boredom can be a major factor in smartphone usage,
but remember you're in charge. You have the power to
stop the habit. There's no need to be dependent on your
phone. Break free, foster a more careful approach with
your cell, and watch your concentration and focus levels
increase and memory and sleep improve. It's not difficult
to take back control. Your health and well-being will
thank you for it.

Overcome your fears

Phone separation anxiety is increasingly becoming an
issue, so much so that there's even a word to describe the
fear of being without your cell phone—nomophobia. For
people who feel this way, the worry arises when they can't
hold their phone in their hand, for example when driving,
or when they're somewhere with a poor signal or the
phone's battery dies. It's a combination of FOMO—the fear
of missing out—along with the often irrational anxiety
that if their phone isn't within reaching distance, an
emergency or disaster will happen.

Sound familiar? The only way to stop your phone
controlling you is to stop relying on it so much and
reacting every time it makes a sound. A party invitation
won't disappear if you wait a day to reply. A review for
a pair of shoes you bought online isn't urgent. Start
learning to let go of the urge to respond to notifications.
Prevent any interruptions by switching your settings, so
you only receive notifications from messaging apps or
other crucial tools, not simply when there's something
new to listen to on a podcast. And when you do hear
that beep, don't abandon what you're doing and let your
phone take priority. You don't need to be immediately
available. Finish the conversation you're having or the task
you're doing—only then pick up your phone. Scarily, the
Deloitte research also highlights that more than half of
smartphone respondents tap at their phone while walking,
with a worrying 11 percent admitting to using them while
crossing the road. It's frightening when a phone takes
priority over personal safety.

It may come as a surprise, but smartphones are only a
decade old and everyone managed fine beforehand. Yes,
cell phones are useful and extremely convenient, but in
days gone by, people were able to function and survive
without any trouble. You can do it too. In fact, you've
probably achieved a few smartphone-free hours during a
flight. Most would agree that it's courteous to keep your
phone out of view—in a purse or pocket—when meeting
people, but what if you turn it off completely? Maybe just
for 30 minutes at first, then for a morning. If it's not a work
phone, you can guarantee you won't have missed much
when you switch it on again. Cue some disappointment
perhaps, but it'll make you realize you can go without.

If you're concerned that family may think you're ignoring them, tell them in advance that you're taking a break from Facebook or that you'll be listening to voicemail messages twice a day. Life will go on. And you'll soon discover it can be a calmer and more satisfied one.

Dependency issues

It's remarkable how much you rely on your cell phone to store family and friends' contact details and addresses. Not so long ago, essential phone numbers had to be committed to memory, but these days that's no longer the case. And it's always been difficult to be able to recall untold addresses. One solution is an old-fashioned address or notebook (there are many gorgeous ones out there). Write down numbers and then manually type them into your phone, rather than tapping on a contacts list photo. Repeat often and the information is more likely to stick.

The same goes for depending on your smartphone as a calendar. Without it, how would you know the date of your next dental appointment, or your niece's birthday? Again, it's handy to have these details in one place and at your fingertips, but what if you were to—heaven forbid—lose your phone or it died on you? Don't take the risk. At least have a diary or paper calendar backup. And there are plenty of beautiful traditional diaries out there.

It's also worthwhile, if you depend on your smartphone to wake you up in the morning, to revert back to a traditional alarm clock. Phones are regular bedfellows— Deloitte discovered that 55 percent of smartphone owners look at their phone within 15 minutes of waking, with a third of UK adults not being able to last more than five minutes without picking up their phone—but did you know that having a cell phone by your bed can be harmful to your health? A bedroom should be a sanctuary, a calm and relaxing space, and a tech-free zone. Nighttime beeps and standby lights are distracting and make for a disturbed night's slumber, while studies show that the blue light emitted from smartphones can upset your internal circadian rhythm, making it harder to fall asleep.

Stop the distractions

Financial budgeting advice, language translators, driving theory tests, BMI calculators—there's an app for everything. While many are enlightening, useful, and assist with productivity, for every Waze or Pocket Yoga app, there's also a Zombies, Run! and Translate for Animals. If you're forever being distracted by apps and find hours vanish with nothing achieved except the next level of Candy Crush or a new outfit for your Bitmoji, then it's time for a major uninstall.

Take a look at all the apps on your smartphone and, if they're not fulfilling a purpose and giving you guidance, inspiration, or factual advice, seriously think about deleting them. Limiting what's on your home screen is a good idea. Anything you use daily can still appear here, but put those travel apps, restaurant guides, and recipes into folders and move to the second and third screens. If they're not always in view, you won't be so tempted to tap on them. After a while of nonusage, you may even decide to delete them.

Take back control

Consider taking social media apps off your phone too. If you often feel compelled to scroll down screen after screen of posts, randomly pressing "like," you're wasting valuable time you could be putting to better use elsewhere. Yes, the cat is cute and it's lovely your colleague is enjoying a cocktail on the beach but, truthfully, your opinion isn't crucial and won't sway an important decision one way or another. Perhaps just take a quick glance at Facebook and Instagram once a week when on your PC or tablet and set yourself a time limit (30 minutes maybe?). Give yourself a break from adding posts, too. The world won't end if you don't share your every thought or move.

It's only when you start taking control and being aware of your daily interaction with your phone that you'll see just how intense your relationship has been. There's no need for a big breakup, though, small steps will make all the difference. Try it.

DARE TO GO NAKED

Enjoy the peace going phoneless can bring

It's a sunny day when I dare to go naked and walk along the beach to the neighboring seaside resort without my phone. Not wanting to take a jacket or carry a bag, it makes sense to leave my cell behind—and pants pockets are way too small for the bulky devices of today. With only the dog in tow, there's no fear of my phone slipping out whenever I bend down to throw a ball, either. Already, worries evaporate.

Tide times are known, so I stroll across the sand. Without constantly checking for texts and emails—even when there are no beeps—my eyes can look out to the horizon, and I see someone on a paddleboard, negotiating the ripples of the sea. He's fixed firm, there's not a wobble, and I note my own posture. Refreshingly, I'm not crouched over for once, my hand isn't cupped and raised to just beneath my nose, I feel several inches taller.

I'm also aware that the promenade is now only a few steps away. The warmth of the sun on my back, and its sparkling rays on the water, transported me for a while to the Greek island I visited last summer. Miles have been gobbled up as my mind has traveled. I see a bench and sit down, next to an older lady. After a few moments, she smiles and asks if my dog is friendly. I assure her he is. We then start to discuss his breed, his unusual name—Chutney—and she recalls memories of her childhood pet. Had I been scrolling through Facebook posts, shopping online, or watching YouTube clips, this conversation may not have happened. The lady's cheery disposition has brightened my day.

She goes on her way, but I remain seated, and although I've been in the same spot many times, my surroundings feel different. My senses seem heightened. I'm observing, hearing and smelling the real world, not once accessed via my phone screen. And in this moment, it's a wonderful place to be. But I don't think I'll announce it to all and sundry via Instagram. This is a treasured time I need only share with Chutney.

DO YOU REMEMBER WHEN...?

Note down memories of special times you've spent without your smartphone

DEMYSTIFYING MEDITATION

There are so many reasons and ways to meditate that it can at first seem daunting, but the benefits of sustained practice are worth the effort. You just need to give it a go

When I began meditating it was a private thing. Nobody I knew meditated and I worried about what other people would think, imagining they might regard me as kookie.

But any potential embarrassment paled into insignificance compared to my overactive mind that refused to be stilled. I was stressed at work and my mind was on constant overdrive, in a state of anxiety and worrying about the smallest things that may or may not happen. It was also holding on to stories of the past, replaying them to justify the way I felt in that moment. It would wake me up in the middle of the night. The whole experience was exhausting. I felt lonely. Guzzling wine at the weekends was my only escape from the life I was leading and the mind that would never rest. Until, of course, I burned out.

Since then a simple, sustainable meditation practice has honestly changed my life and I truly believe anyone can benefit from it. I don't see meditation as the answer or a fix but instead a vehicle to slow down and check in with myself. In this space I know and understand myself better and can make choices that are more aligned to what serves me best. It has ultimately led me to creating a life I love.

To begin with, it can be helpful to break meditation down and view it afresh. Here's how....

FIVE TIPS FOR NEW MEDITATORS

1. There is no one way
There are many approaches, theories, and philosophies when it comes to meditation. At the start, these can seem overwhelming. If you have already tried meditation and found it difficult, it is important to know that this is completely normal and to be expected. People are complex creatures. But rather than give up before you have begun, instead explore different types of meditation as a way to get to know yourself a little better. What works for one person may not work for another. Try movement meditations such as yoga, t'ai chi, or breathing techniques (pranayama) or explore different guided meditations online or in a class. They are all equally valid and effective.

2. Thoughts are completely normal
We live busy, complicated lives that involve attending to myriad tasks, solving problems, and looking after family members. So when you sit down to meditate, especially for the first time, do not be surprised when your mind wanders almost immediately. The art of meditation is noticing when your mind has taken a different direction and bringing it back to your focus.

3. You cannot do it wrong
See your meditation practice as time and space just for you. In the moments of quiet, you are free of life's complications and challenges. You can let go of the roles and responsibilities with which you identify yourself. You will most likely have meditated naturally in everyday life at times but might not realize you were doing it. Unless you are following a structured path or approach to meditation, I believe you cannot ever do it wrong. You have to start somewhere— if that is just a few seconds of quiet, a feeling of deep relaxation, being free of distractions, or a calming of thought you are meditating.

4. It takes patient practice
Western science now proves what Eastern philosophies have taught for centuries—taking time each day to sit quietly to simply breathe, listen to your surroundings and your heart, and quieten your mind has enormous physiological and psychological benefits and can lead to a heightened sense of general well-being. In today's fast-paced society taking time to be still is more important than ever. We remember to look after our bodies, other people, even our homes but often forget to look after our minds. The long-term benefits of meditation do not happen overnight, so be patient. Science and any long-term meditator will tell you the practice is worth it.

5. It is for anyone and everyone
You do not need to believe a certain thing, dress a certain way, or have a certain outlook on life to benefit from meditation. Whether you are a chief executive trying to manage the pressures of running a company or a busy parent seeking to handle family challenges (or both) meditation is for you. Similarly, it does not matter if you are simply looking for a way to balance your emotions or you are a spiritual person hoping to deepen your connection to that which is greater than us... all are welcome. See meditation as yours—your mind, your meditation. Whether that is being more mindful in everyday life, carving out a few minutes each day to simply breathe with more awareness, or a more formal practice, it is for you.

The essence of health

Many people may seem outwardly well, but scratch the surface and there is often disharmony, sadness, and self-loathing. The practice of yoga, which unites mind and body, could pave the way to a healthier, happier life

How do you define the state of being healthy? Does it mean having smooth skin, a trim waistline, and a within-range BMI? Or is it better defined by a calm mind, a kind disposition, and a happy attitude? Perhaps it's one or a combination of these things. The cut-and-dried perspective of "do my numbers look okay at my yearly checkup?" is one way of measuring it, yet this doesn't get at the emotional, sublime aspect of health: your own intuitive sense of well-being. Despite many attempts to find a litmus test for health, at least in the Western medical world, we still haven't found one simple gold standard to measure it.

I'm a medical doctor who has been an emergency physician for more than 14 years and have seen my fair share of both acute and chronic disease. I've met many people who, at first glance, might fall under the category of unhealthy: People who come to me because their kidneys are not working effectively, or they have chest pain, or they can't breathe well. Yet, as I delve deeper into their spirit and work with them, I see a whole other face of health. Despite having renal, heart, or lung disease, the person in front of me is calm and happy with a legacy of accomplishments.

On the flip side, though, every day in the store, at the post office, or at the bank, I see an outwardly healthy person with no obvious medical list who is full of sadness and self-loathing. They don't have an inner peace and become infuriated if delayed by only a few moments standing in line while an assistant counts out their change.

I bring up these juxtapositions to illustrate the point that health must first and foremost come from a place of unity of mind and body, a place of perspective. This intuitive awareness, cultivated through yoga and other mindfulness practices, offers the ability to pause, take note, and reflect on how you feel, behave, and react to a situation—and how you make choices. With this groundwork in place, you can make effective choices in all aspects of life—from the foods you eat, the exercise you take, the sleep with which you restore yourself—and move toward a healthy, long and rewarding life.

The research is in

As well as emergency medicine, I've been practicing yoga for more than 25 years and, as a certified Yoga Medicine instructor, focus on the fusion of anatomy, physiology, and biomechanics with the traditional practice of yoga. In practicing and teaching yoga, I've felt the synergy of the yoking of mind and body and the deep calm and happiness that have come as a result of my dedicated practice. Many of my students have had similar experiences. Can yoga help us to be healthier? Anecdotally, I say yes but, as a scientist, I also say, "let's turn to the literature..."

A 2009 study in *BMC Pulmonary Medicine*, by Vempati et al, looked at 57 adults with mild to moderate asthma. Twenty-nine of these participants were randomized to a yoga group and 28 to a non-yoga

"My practice has given me the perspective to realize that when I'm feeling sad or defeated, this feeling will not be forever and I will learn and grow from the experience"

group. The yoga group showed statistically significant improvement in pulmonary function, a decrease in exercise-induced broncho-constriction, and overall improvement in quality of life.

A review in *Preventative Medicine* in December 2017, by Thind et al, analyzed a group of studies assessing the effects of yoga on lowering blood sugar in participants with Type 2 diabetes. In addition to the yoga group showing an improvement in blood sugar metrics, they also showed improvements in lipid profile, blood pressure, body mass index, waist/hip ratio, and cortisol levels.

In April 2017, in the *Journal of Complementary and Alternative Medicine*, Chu et al looked at the effect a 12-week yoga program had on heart rate variability (HRV)—a marker of parasympathetic tone—and depressive symptoms in clinically depressed women. Thirteen women were included in the yoga group and 13 in the non-yoga group. The yoga group completed a 12-week yoga program where they participated in twice-weekly, 60-minute yoga classes. Each session consisted of breathing exercises, a yoga pose practice, and supine meditation and relaxation.

The control group was instructed not to engage in any yoga practice and to maintain their usual level of physical activity during the course of the study. All participants' HRV, depressive symptoms, and perceived stress were assessed at baseline and post-test. The authors found that the 12-week yoga program was effective in increasing parasympathetic tone and reducing depressive symptoms and perceived stress in women with elevated depressive symptoms.

Greater acceptance of yoga

This small sampling of studies suggests yoga promotes good health. But in what way? The truth is that this area of research is in its infancy. The sizes of many of the studies are small, some of the methods are less than robust and because there's so much variability of yoga styles and practice, it's difficult to make a direct correlation between yoga and improvement in health outcomes. But there is great momentum and it's likely that more robust studies will emerge in the near future.

Over the past 40 years the medical community has begun to acknowledge the overall positive benefits of yoga, and mindfulness practices have also been increasingly accepted. Many researchers are interested in growing the body of knowledge that explains what it is about these practices that makes people healthier. In fact, the University of Massachusetts Medical School recently created a new division dedicated to the academic study of mindfulness. Such a designation allows for long-term, hopefully better-funded, focused research.

Mental flexibility

Back to anecdote… In my years as an emergency physician, I've dealt with many things that were out of my control to fix. I have experienced the joy of bringing people back from the brink. Yet many times all I can say is: "I don't know." The stress, trauma, jubilation, and sadness that are all parts of my job are hard to manage for many who have the privilege of caring for the very sick. I've continually turned to my practice to give me the mental flexibility to think clearly when I need to make quick decisions. My practice has given me the perspective to realize that when I'm feeling tired or sad or defeated, this feeling will not be forever and I will learn and grow from the experience. In my times of complete physical and mental exhaustion, it has been my salvation—a place to find physical strength, mental balance and a state of "reset." In essence, my practice has made me a better doctor and healthier person.

I've seen similar spaciousness grow in the hearts, minds, and bodies of my students. As their practices have unfolded and they have developed a sense of peace, nonreactivity, physical strength, flexibility, and mobility, many have made major life changes. They have repaired relationships, made fulfilling career decisions, become physically fitter, and said no to things that weren't working in their lives. They are happier, healthier, and whole. The vibe in my studio is one of inclusion where much of the goodness occurs in the lobby with students sharing, laughing, connecting. This is the essence of health.

To find a Yoga Medicine certified instructor in your area, visit yogamedicine.com.

Words: **Doctor Amy Sedgwick MD**
Amy is a Yoga Medicine instructor based in Portland, Maine, where she practices emergency medicine. Her Riverbend Yoga and Meditation Studio helps people achieve holistic wellness from within.

ILLUSTRATION: IRINA DALZIEL

MIND THE GAP
The art of staying put

Do you sometimes feel like your life would be so much better if only you had a bigger house, a better job, or more friends? Here's how to stop wanting more and find the happiness you've been looking for in the here and now

WHERE YOU
WANT TO BE

WHERE YOU
ARE NOW

Have you ever found yourself browsing real estate websites despite no particular plans to move house? How about Googling unrealistic careers in search of that elusive dream job? Or perhaps, like me, you've spent an inordinate amount of time researching the best family-friendly dog breeds and poring over images of Scandinavian-inspired interiors on Pinterest.

It's surprising how much you can learn about your life goals from a quick glance at your internet browser history. When engaged in this kind of research, it's easy to justify it as self-improvement or harmless fantasy. But this constant craving for a new, improved life carries an implicit message: that life is not okay just as it is. And this goal-orientated mode of thinking can chip away at well-being.

Firstly, it turns the focus of attention away from all the wonderful things you do have and toward the gap between where you are now and where you want to be, which can lead to a constant gnawing sense of dissatisfaction. Secondly, it tends to be driven by an underlying belief that once those goals are attained, life will really begin, as though life were a finite wish list with happiness waiting at the end: "If I get a bigger house... then I'll be happy." "If I get a new job... then I'll be happy."

A bigger house, a better job, or an adorable puppy might deliver a short-term dose of pleasure—even a momentary release from the constant craving—but when engaged in this mode of striving, awareness of the present moment is restricted. Even if those long-awaited goals are attained, you'll likely be too busy focusing on the next goal to fully appreciate them.

The comparison crisis

Today's digitally driven culture doesn't help. If it's not the internet, drawing you in with its promise of a better life at the click of a mouse, it's social media. The edited highlights of other people's lives become unrealistic benchmarks against which to measure happiness and success. And they are unrealistic: When was the last time you saw an Instagram picture of someone washing the dishes or arguing with their partner?

"Online media can change your goals without you realizing," says Gemma Griffith, director of postgraduate programs at Bangor University's Centre for Mindfulness Research and Practice in the UK. "When you see other people with seemingly better lives, jobs, partners, and houses it widens the gap between where you are and where you think you ought to be.

"The goalposts get moved and you can become dissatisfied with your life by seeing the highlights of the lives of others."

The discrepancy monitor

This sense of insatiable wanting has been around a lot longer than Facebook. In Buddhist teaching, it is seen as greed, one of the three main causes of human suffering or Three Poisons (greed, hatred, and delusion). This focus on the gap between what is and what is desired is a key theme of modern mindfulness-based teachings. Termed "discrepancy-based processing" or "monitoring," it's seen as a product of what is known as the "doing" mode of mind.

"Humans are experts in discrepancy-based processing, it is how we get things done," says Gemma. "For example, I might be aware that I need to buy some bread. There is now a gap between how things are (no bread) and what I want (bread). I know how to bridge this gap by going to the store. Once I have bought the bread, I have achieved my goal and I can tick it off my to-do list and let it go."

The trouble begins when the mind becomes locked in "doing" mode and this discrepancy-focused mindset is applied to goals that can't be attained, or to internal weather patterns, such as moods and feelings. "If we're feeling sad, we notice a gap between where we are right now [sad] and where we want to be [happy]," adds Gemma. "We can do things that we think will make us happy to bring us closer to our goal, such as go to a party, but when the party is over, are we any closer to happiness?

"The discrepancy-based processing is activated and, in doing mode, you try to 'solve' the problem of sadness. But unlike the task of buying bread, this can't simply be ticked off a to-do list. This results in a constant monitoring of the gap, and if a mismatch is found this can make you feel worse. Then, as you ruminate on why you're sad, you make yourself feel even lower."

Don't do, just be

It doesn't have to be like this. There is a way to escape the shackles of the doing mode of mind, to let go of this exhausting and insatiable desire for things to be different and to embrace things just the way they are. And it doesn't involve burning your laptop and smartphone. In fact, it involves doing very little—other than noticing when the mind is in this potentially harmful mode and gently escorting the attention to what is happening right now. Cue: the "being" mode.

In their book *Mindfulness-Based Cognitive Therapy for Depression*, MBCT founders Zindel Segal, Mark Williams, and John Teasdale explain that doing and being are the two main modes of mind or mental gears: "The being mode is not devoted to achieving particular goals. In this mode, there is no need to emphasize discrepancy-based processing or constantly to monitor and evaluate ('How am I doing in meeting my goals?'). Instead, the focus of the being mode is accepting and allowing what is, without any immediate pressure to change it."

Likening these modes to the gears of a car, the authors go on to suggest that the mind can only be engaged in one gear at a time. By consciously shifting gears from doing to being mode, the former is naturally disabled and the mind set free from its tyranny. Mindfulness-based courses, such as MBCT, use techniques to train the mind to move from doing to being mode, and there are also exercises you can try at home. Hopefully it will help to bring happiness to your doorstep.

Next time you find yourself ruminating about the future, try the exercises below...

FOUR STEPS TO MOVE FROM "DOING" TO "BEING"

1 Notice
The first step to disengaging from doing mode is to notice when you're caught in its vise-like grip. Unfortunately, one of the key traits of this mental gear is it tends to thrive when you're on autopilot. As such, you can spend long periods of time scrolling through Facebook or daydreaming, without even realising you're doing it. The more you practice, the more adept you will become at catching yourself in this mode. For now, try setting up a reminder system by placing stickers where you know they'll be seen throughout the day, such as on your computer or the refrigerator door. Each time you see a sticker, ask yourself the question: What mode of mind am I in right now?

2 Come back to the present
When you've caught yourself in "doing" mode, change gear by gently bringing the mind back to the present. Take a moment to pause and get a sense of the body right here, right now, focusing on the sensation of the feet on the ground. Note any thoughts, feelings, or physical sensations that are present: What is happening for you right now? When you're ready, turn your attention to the breath. Take at least five conscious breaths, following each one all the way in and all the way out, as an anchor to the present. Next, widen your field of attention to include the body as a whole, as though the whole body were breathing.

3 Take a moment of gratitude
Before you go back to your daily activities, use this pause as an opportunity to appreciate what you have in your life. Bring to mind three things for which you're grateful. This could be the roof over your head, the stable job you have, or your family and good friends. Think of someone with whom you have shared happy moments or someone who has supported you and been there for you. Taking time to stop and reflect can help you to appreciate what you have and to re-evaluate what really makes you happy. It could also uncover what's less important—particularly useful if you've just spent the past hour trawling the internet to find the perfect cushion for your new couch.

4 Swap longing for living
Instead of yearning for a happy future, discover joy right now. Every time you catch yourself reaching for your phone to scroll through your social media feeds make a conscious choice to seize the moment and spend the time doing something nourishing—an activity that is guaranteed to make you feel good. Dance around to your favorite song, read a thought-provoking article, get creative, take a bath. As John Kabat-Zinn says in his best-selling mindfulness tome *Full Catastrophe Living*: "...the present moment, whenever it is recognized and honored, reveals a very special, indeed magical power: it is the only time that any of us ever has."

Serenity
and the city

*Bustling conurbations don't have to leave
you feeling frazzled. Losing yourself in
a crowd can be the ultimate getaway*

New York, the city that never sleeps. A city of 8.5 million
people—plus more than 60 million tourists each year.
Like many of these visitors, I'd gone in search of bright
lights and big sights. I certainly wasn't anticipating a
peaceful retreat. Yet somehow, after elbowing my way out
of the subway on my first day, that's exactly what I found.

Oddly enough, it was work that led me to the realization
that cities aren't all hustle and bustle. They can be places
of rest, too. Emerging that sunny October morning in
Manhattan, I battled on through the crowds—and the
heavy fug of jet lag—looking for somewhere that I could
send an important email (not a fire-it-off-on-your-phone
kind of message). I walked past a few cafés—all full,
all irritatingly loud—before chancing upon New York
Public Library on 5th Avenue. My expectations weren't
high. I sighed as I saw the line at the security desk, then
the groups of chit-chatty tourists congregating on the
stairs to admire the building's Beaux-Arts beauty. Then I
reached the Rose Main Reading Room, all grand wooden
desks and low-hanging lamps. It was just the place to get
down to business. I got out my laptop, logged onto the
free wifi, and dutifully tapped out my email.

But I stayed much longer. Not to carry on working,
but to take it all in—the respectful hush of the room;
the unspoken solidarity; the dreamy frescos on the
ceiling; the walls lined with old books. There was also the
tempting fantasy that I was an undergraduate again—a
student, at Harvard or Yale probably, in one of those
college movies. *Good Will Hunting, Legally Blonde...*

Spaces in between

Following my imaginative adventures at the library,
I started to see the city—and my trip—differently. I
allowed myself to get lost in the crowds and I stopped to
look closer. I sought out cramped backstreet bookstores;
vast, intimidating museums; and the small, quiet spaces
in between. There was a corporate courtyard with a
mesmerizing water feature, the bounty of a cared-for
community garden, and a street full of flower sellers
wilting in the after-lunch slump.

With this slow, mindful type of travel taking over,
I realized I was also seeking out different activities—
restorative yoga classes, meditation walks, and creative
writing workshops. I even took in a comedy show, where
I reveled in being a passive member of the audience,
happily disguised by the darkness. Of course, I could

have done many of these things outside of the city, but this packed scene offered them all up conveniently in one place. That's one of the unique perks of an urban retreat.

Digital detox

Let's begin at check-in. Many hotels and spas in urban areas are now encouraging guests to unwind after a long day of travel, work, or sightseeing by braving a digital detox. The James Hotel NoMad in New York, for instance, will give you 10 percent off your bill every night you go tech-free. Guests hand over their phone and other electronic devices at the reception desk, before being shown to a room that's been stripped of all digital distractions—no TV, laptop, or even alarm clock. Hedon Spa & Hotel in the city of Pärnu, Estonia, offers totally silent spa sessions. It's a trend taking off in urban spas

worldwide, as predicted at the Global Wellness Summit in its report, *8 Wellness Trends for 2017—and Beyond*. And there are mindful eating restaurants on the way, too.

Cities are also hubs for yoga and meditation, so whatever helps you unplug—silent yin, candlelit flow, or kundalini—you're more likely to find it in a city than in the countryside. The city of Vancouver is renowned for its yoga offerings, hosting an ever-evolving program of classes, top teachers, and meditation sessions. You can sometimes take advantage of being an out-of-towner with a free trial, too. And, in truth, you may need those mindfulness skills on the busy bus ride home.

After hours

A good way to experience the more serene side to city life is either to get up early or go out late. Aim to see it off-peak, at times when most people will be sleeping, working, or doing the opposite of what you're doing.

Wherever you are in the world, it's always a treat to watch the sun rise. If you can, see the city wake up from above. Even in a metropolis as frenetic and traffic-mad as LA, there's a quiet time. The Griffith Observatory may not be open at first light, but you can still find a vantage point. Go on a short walk up one of Beverly Hills' illustrious peaks or pack a breakfast smoothie and take a hike in the San Fernando Valley—those golden California panoramas will be yours alone (give or take a few super-fit power walkers).

Anonymity is bliss

Nighttime also offers new perspectives on a city. Many museums and galleries have evening openings, and some stay open all night on occasion. In London, Tate Modern is open every Friday and Saturday until 10pm, while the National Portrait Gallery runs popular Friday Lates, with drop-in drawing classes and live DJs. Alternatively, awaken your curiosity at one of the Silent Nights at Dennis Severs' House. Located at 18 Folgate Street in Spitalfields, its candlelit rooms have been reimagined to document the lives and changing fortunes of a family of Huguenot silk-weavers. Each room, with its distinct sights, sounds and smells, gives the impression that a mysterious person has just left the space. Immersed in this 18th-century world, you'll be oblivious to the trendy toing and froing outside.

An escape to the city doesn't necessarily need to be about finding a quiet corner where there aren't many people. Another appeal is its anonymity. When no one knows your name, who you are or where you come from, you're free to be, well, whoever you want to be. There are no questions to field from (mostly) well-meaning loved ones and no expectations about what you should be wearing, eating, doing, or even thinking.

Choose a city—the bigger, the better—and embrace the masses. Try Paris. Skip along the Champs-Élysées. Dance your way up the Eiffel Tower and daydream your way around Notre-Dame. Who cares if people stare? After all, you never have to see them again.

Then there's Tokyo—one of the largest cities in the world. Here, unless you speak Japanese, your anonymity is likely to be even further enhanced. Do things no one would expect of you back home: Eat giant heaps of sushi for breakfast, watch sumo at the Ryōgoku Kokugikan arena, go wild on the rides at Tokyo Disneyland.

Escape the countryside

If all this has you curious, and you'd like to give it a try, choose a city close to home for your first experience. Book a hotel for a night or two (many offer great savings on Sunday-night stays) or just make it a day trip. You don't have to travel far to dip into the restorative benefits of a city escape.

You could reignite your spark with an evening at the theater, whether it's a thought-provoking play or a laughter-inducing farce. Then stimulate your palate at an amazing restaurant—eating alone will focus your senses on the textures and tastes on your plate—and maybe top it all off with a stay at a plush hotel. If possible, choose somewhere special with a bed that's much larger and more luxurious than you have at home—it will feel like a real retreat.

When escaping the countryside, it might be helpful to remember the beginner's meditation mantra: whatever comes, let it be. You can choose to focus on it, or you can just let it pass.

GET THE MOST OUT OF YOUR TIME IN THE CITY

- Since you'll never totally silence the city, you can at least mute your smartphone. Avoid annoying distractions by keeping your phone on airplane mode as much as possible.
- Even in a city you know well, there are often areas you've never visited and whole communities with cuisines and traditions that might be unfamiliar. Veer off from your own beaten track and be open to something different.
- Pack a swimsuit and head to a lido or rooftop pool in your chosen city. The feeling of floating on water, gazing up at the sky, is practically synonymous with peace and tranquility.

The urban jungle

Mindful ways to bring nature to your city door

Forest bathing—the therapy that prescribes an immersion among trees in order to improve one's emotional well-being—seems an unnecessary invention. Everyone knows that being in nature is good for you, especially when city life can be stressful. And yet that stress means there's little headspace to plan nature into your life: Ironically, because the outdoors can give you the mental clarity you need. Forest bathing provides a guide for overloaded urbanites to access the green spaces beyond a city's suburbs.

I'm all for a plan to help keep mental and physical health intact—and I know that walking through woodland is good for my soul. But for those who live in the middle of cities, getting to the nearest forest is a considerable undertaking. It requires time and transport and, although I adore walking among spring bluebells and fall leaves, a six-monthly stroll through the trees is nowhere near enough to ease the pressures of city life.

I also think that regular contact with nature is more important than an occasional total immersion—and not only for the peace of mind it brings. Fresh air and natural light first thing help to reset the body's circadian rhythm, aiding a restful night's sleep. In addition, unhooking yourself from the morning phone-check delays any potential stress response.

THE QUICK-FIX CITY-STYLE ALTERNATIVE TO FOREST BATHING

Do you live within walking distance of a park? If not, discover some nearby trees. Even sidewalk-planted ones provide a nature hit. Start the following once a week, perhaps on a day off. Then, set your alarm early and go outside several times a week.

1 Wake up early. Get up, get dressed, and head outside. Don't check your phone. Just go.

2 Walk to the place you've chosen. It should be around a 10-minute stroll.

3 Enter the park or nature spot. Choose a tree and place your hands upon it, if you're feeling brave. If not, take a few moments to study the tree closely. Notice the patterns made by the bark and the branches. What shape are the leaves? Try to spend at least a minute there, absorbing your surroundings. Breathe.

4 Then, when you're ready, return home and continue with your day.

I was out of my comfort zone the first time I took a dawn-lit trip to place my hands on a tree, joggers and dog walkers nearby. But then I realized that the peace and headspace it gave me was worth it. Nature moves at its own pace and stops you speeding too fast for your own good. Adopting a regular urban alternative to forest bathing reminds me there's more to life than the dizzying confluence of thoughts racing about my mind.

So remember: No one needs the grandeur of a forest immersion to get the benefits of nature. Just by creating a regular practice, close to home, you'll sleep better, slow down, and feel calmness all around.

INTO THE BLUE

Why does the ocean have that calming effect?

Seeking solace by a waterfront is something many people have done. When you're depleted or stressed or simply wanting to gather your thoughts, a walk in the woods can be wonderful but a stroll by the sea somehow seems to clear the air just a little more powerfully. As it turns out, this sense of calm that washes over you as you stand by the open ocean, a sprawling lake, or even a trickling stream is not imagined. That deep feeling of peace, that shifting of consciousness, that strength and excitement for life is what marine biologist, best-selling author, and protector of the seas, Wallace J. Nichols, calls Blue Mind—a new discovery in the emerging field of neuroconservation.

What is Blue Mind?

"Blue Mind describes the mildly meditative state characterized by calm, peacefulness, unity, and a sense of general happiness and satisfaction with life in the moment," explains Wallace, a man known as "Keeper of the Sea" for his understanding and work based on the water that makes up most of the planet.

"Blue Mind is inspired by water and elements associated with water, from the color blue to the words we use to describe the sensations associated with immersion. It takes advantage of neurological connections formed over millennia, many such brain patterns and preferences being discovered only now thanks to innovative scientists and cutting-edge technology."

In a world where so many experience daily exhaustion, screen fatigue, and anxiety, which in turn can lead to chronic illness, insomnia, and often an over-reliance on drugs and alcohol to unwind, Blue Mind could offer a connection to a deep health and well-being boost that taps into ancient neural pathways.

Wallace's research into neuroconservation through his project Blue Mind, named for the combination of two scientific conversations—one being the future and exploration of waters, lakes, rivers, and oceans, and the other the golden age of neuroscience research right now—suggests that being by water (even a bath at home) has the potential to alleviate cognitive conditions and physical ailments. This discovery could offer new insight into the human psyche and the healing qualities of water.

The research, which is led by Wallace, is conducted by neuropsychologists who use a range of methods: From simple data collection through interviews, surveys, and questionnaires to measuring stress hormones in saliva, monitoring breathing and heart rates, and measuring electrical activity (EEG) and oxygen flow (fMRI) to the brain as subjects engage with a variety of activities and stimuli. The results show that human beings have a natural predisposition to be soothed by bodies of water, offering what Wallace says are profound implications for how people take care of themselves and the blue planet in this "golden age of exploration of both our brains and our wild waters."

Blue Mind versus Red Mind

As well as the overall cognitive and physical benefits of being by water, research into Blue Mind has shed further light on why this act of wellness is something that is desperately needed by people all over the world. It would appear that humans, as a species, have switched into what neuroscientists call Red Mind on a day-to-day basis—

something that is quite the opposite of Blue Mind and can be detrimental to health.

Red Mind is what Wallace describes as "an edgy high, characterized by stress, anxiety, fear, and maybe even a little bit of anger and despair." A result of the physiological fight-or-flight response that evolved to help us survive, Red Mind has wound up being the go-to brain setting for inappropriate situations. This is believed to be a reaction to the bombardment of constant information and a way of living not conducive to humans' biological needs.

"These days we're in Red Mind mode a lot," says Wallace. "Information streams in from around the world, demanding our attention. We're more distracted, anxious, and stressed than ever. Left unchecked that Red Mind becomes Gray Mind: a numbed-out, indifferent, listless and depressive state." He adds: "Stress and anxiety can cause or exacerbate many diseases, disorders, and unhealthy conditions. The stress hormone, cortisol, is known to promote inflammation which impedes healing. Activities that remove or reduce stress, such as taking time to be by water, can complement health care."

"We let our minds wander and dream. Waterside is a place for play, romance, a sense of peace and freedom, contemplation, grieving, and remembering"

Indeed, being on, in, or even near water has now been proven to imbue the senses, help to quieten and still overactive minds, and even balance hormones. It also helps us to tap into insight, creativity, and compassion that might otherwise be suppressed.

"To tap into our Blue Mind, we must close down the screens, log out, stand up, and walk outside," explains Wallace. "From here, we travel until we glimpse the water, then move closer until we're at its edge. We can walk along its shores, climb onto a boat or board, or strip down and submerge. Here, the auditory, visual, and somatic processing is simplified. Assuming we'll feel comfortable and safe, our minds and bodies can be restored. Our brain switches into a different mode where creativity, insight, and connections with others are enhanced. We are open to the experiences of awe and wonder which can boost empathy and compassion. Our breathing and heart rate tends to slow down. We let our minds wander and dream. Waterside is a place for play, romance, a sense of peace and freedom, contemplation, grieving, and remembering."

The magic and importance of allowing yourself to experience Blue Mind on a regular basis becomes clear.

Welcome Blue Mind into daily life

Blue Mind is something that everyone can benefit from, both emotionally and physically. Better yet, spreading awareness of how integral the ocean and other waterways are to life will help to support marine conservation efforts worldwide. Tapping into Blue Mind is a natural form of self-care from which you can immediately reap rewards. All you need is water.

How to be present by the sea

Ready to experience the wonders of Blue Mind? Once you have made your way to your chosen body of water (the sea, an open lake, a pond) and found a quiet spot, reaping the benefits that stem from the sights, sounds, smells, and even the energy of the water is as easy as just being there. But being is sometimes harder than it should be when the mind is filled with distracting thoughts. The key is to become present in the moment.

Being present always begins and comes back to breathing, a constant in life, but one that often goes unnoticed. Bringing awareness to the breath helps to clear the mind and release anxiety—the first steps toward being present in the moment. Mouth-breathing triggers a subtle anxiety response, so the trick with deliberate and focused breath is to take a deep, steady inhalation and then release it slowly through the nose, focusing on nothing but the process at hand.

Continue this conscious breathing. Don't try to suppress or ignore distracting thoughts that enter your head. Instead, hear them, acknowledge them, and then deliberately let them pass, always coming back to the breath and what is going on in the moment. The goal is to reach a place in the mind and body that is accepting of everything around, internally and externally. Cling to nothing. Exist, let go, and be with the water.

TAP INTO BLUE MIND AT HOME

You don't have to be by the sea to find your Blue Mind. In fact, you don't even have to leave your house, if you don't want to. Here are Wallace's tips for bringing Blue Mind into your home...

- Make time for a long luxurious bath each week with the door locked, lights out, bath salts, candles, perhaps a glass of wine.
- Add a small fountain indoors or outside and take time out of your busy life to sit, listen, and contemplate.
- Turn off the TV or radio news and instead, listen to calming water sounds. This is also a wonderful way to help you drift off into a peaceful sleep.
- Hang water-themed artwork on the walls of your home as a permanent reminder of the beauty and calm of our blue planet.

WORDS: RUBY DEEVOY. PHOTOGRAPHS: DAVID BAKER

Facing your fears

Everyone has fears, but when they start affecting the decisions you make and stop you living your life the way you want to, it's time to face up to them. A little hard work and a willingness to step outside your comfort zone can help you conquer your anxiety and reach your greatest potential

Most people have goals and aims—hopes and dreams of the things they want to get out of life; that perfect job they'd love to do; the once-in-a lifetime experience they've dreamed of since childhood; or even just making a habit of a simple action that might mean their day-to-day life is a little healthier.

Sometimes though, the things you want (or need) to do feel scary and out of reach. There are generally two ways of dealing with this: running away—effectively burying your head in the sand and doing nothing to change the situation—or diving in head first, facing the fear head-on. Although the latter strategy works for some, for others it may only serve to magnify the issue, making it even more scary. This can exacerbate the fear and push the likelihood of overcoming it farther away. But what if there was a middle path? A way to swim with the tide, rather than fighting your way through stomach-churning waves? The good news is that there is a way.

First, it's worth asking why people develop fears at all. Sophie Sabbage, author of *Lifeshocks*, has worked with thousands of clients, helping them to resource themselves with the life skills they need to enjoy more peaceful and fulfilled lives, run successful businesses and gain confidence by overcoming their fears. Sophie uses the acronym "False Evidence Appearing Real" to describe fear. "Many are based on things we tell ourselves about something, or what we believe will happen if we do something, or what we believe about ourselves—most of which is profoundly false," she says.

This mind-talk, as Sophie calls it, often develops as a result of beliefs people pick up from a young age, "...usually in response to a lifeshock—a moment in time when our perception of how we see life collides with how life actually is." For example, you may have told yourself you're useless after making a simple mistake as a child, and this creates a fearful state of being which can run your life. But it is possible to take control of your thinking and dispel the myths you have created about yourself. As Sophie explains: "We can challenge and change what we think, and that's a very empowering thing."

Danger signals

Claire Taylor is a small business owner who had struggled with a fear of speaking in public—something that is shared by many people—for as long as she could remember. "It was just the thought of my brain freezing and that I wouldn't know what to say," she explains. "I didn't want to be embarrassed, so it stopped me from doing so many things I had wanted to do."

It seems Claire's reaction is a natural human response to facing a fear, as registered psychologist Rachel Hard explains: "There is an entire section of our brain that is on the lookout for danger. It is an adaptive process that results in a fight, flight, or freeze response—protective mechanisms that help keep us safe." Claire's fears interpreted public speaking as dangerous, creating a state of anxiety whenever she thought about it. When such feelings arise it's all too easy to spiral into a state of negative rumination which, in turn, creates more drama around the source of the anxiety. This makes the problem feel bigger, the fear more scary, and therefore the prospect of facing the fear less likely.

As Sophie said, the irony is that these fears are usually not even true, but people behave as though they are. So a seemingly innocuous case of pronouncing a word incorrectly, or not knowing the answer to a question at school, might embed a belief in a child's mind that they cannot be trusted to say the right thing, triggering a lifelong dialogue of negative mind-talk.

For Claire, there came a point when she had to confront the issue: "I'd recently started my own business and knew I would need to present publicly to help this succeed."

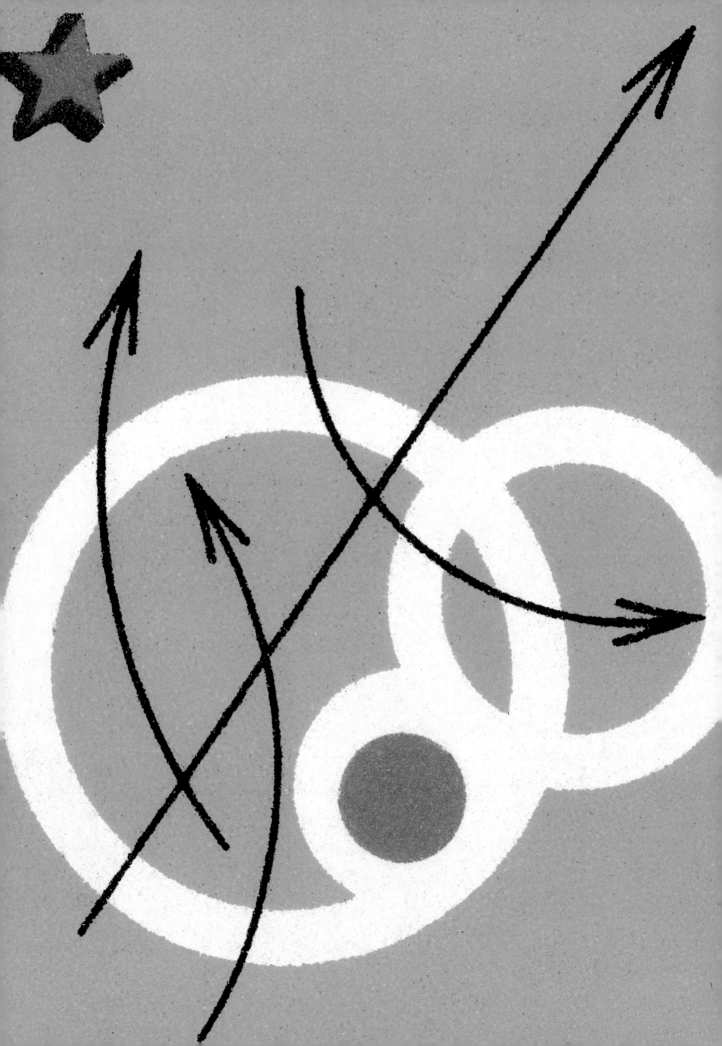

"Bringing an element of fun to an otherwise challenging situation can help to distract attention from the fear, resulting in a positive state"

It wasn't, then, just a challenge to overcome but—as with so many other people and their respective fears—something that had to be managed in order to move forward with life.

How did Claire do this? "I had completed a one-day business presentation course but felt it didn't give me any practice, which is what I thought I needed. Someone then suggested stand-up comedy lessons, saying they often helped corporate clients looking to develop presenting skills."

It sounds like a radical, though creative, way of managing something scary. But bringing an element of fun to an otherwise challenging situation can help to distract attention from the fear, resulting in a more positive emotional state. "I signed up for an eight-week course," recalls Claire. "It was great fun learning to write my own material—rather than focusing purely on presenting, which is the thing that scared me."

"People are generally able to identify what makes them fearful, so exploring and reframing their thoughts can help them to see that just because they think that something might happen, the situation or object itself isn't actually scary," says Rachel. "By slowly challenging their thoughts they have the chance to see that in reality they can manage." In Claire's case she was able to challenge her thoughts and change how she felt, disproving her belief that she would embarrass herself if she spoke in public. She gained confidence that she did know what she was talking about—she was able to dispel this myth by writing her own material, and making a conscious choice to speak in public.

Turn fear into excitement

Jo Bidmead, a volunteer co-ordinator and yoga teacher, was terrified of moths until she reached her early 20s. "It all started when my sister locked me in an outside toilet at my grandad's house when I was five years old. There were huge moths flying around and I felt they were going to hurt me."

This created a belief in Jo's young mind that moths were dangerous, a notion that continued until a friend helped her to challenge it by seeing the creatures in a different way. "My friend encouraged me to see them as beautiful eyelashes coming toward me. After that I was able to see the moths as they truly were and not to attach them to the story of being shut in a scary place. So now I love them as much as butterflies."

Jo also learned some helpful words that might help others through otherwise scary situations: "When I get scared or anxious about anything I say to myself: 'Fear is just excitement without breath.'" This is true; the fight, flight, or freeze response that Rachel described earlier invokes physiological effects that include an increased heart rate, raised blood pressure, and shallow, rapid breathing. Regulating the breath is a fast and simple way to shift the body—and mind—to a more relaxed and calm state, much better for facing your fears.

Of Claire's foray into the world of comedy? "I presented my routine at a graduation comedy night to about 150 people. I was nervous, but it went down really well and I felt such a relief once it was over. I think now I've done that I can actually do anything." Public speaking now forms a large part of Claire's job as she travels the world presenting at seminars and major events. Life-changing indeed.

There are strategies that can help you to face your fears and who knows, the results might just change your life. Try it for yourself and experience the satisfaction of doing it your way.

STRATEGIES TO OVERCOME THE FEAR

- **Accept:** This is a challenging situation for you, and that's okay. There's nothing to be embarrassed about or ashamed of—everyone has fears. Congratulate yourself on being open to overcoming this.
- **Explore:** Brainstorm your thoughts; verbally or, even better, write them down. What messages have you been telling yourself? Can you identify where they came from, when they started, and any triggers?
- **Challenge:** Step back; view these thoughts and beliefs as an observer. Ask yourself are they really true?
- **Team up:** Seek support from a friend, a group, or a therapist with proven expertise in helping people to overcome the issue if you feel you need more specialized help.
- **Normalize:** How can you make this a part of everyday life? Look for ways to make it fun or enjoyable, as Claire and Jo did.
- **Be kind:** Show yourself some compassion and give yourself a break. Start small and go gently. Be open to making mistakes; things don't have to be perfect.
- **Breathe:** Remember to breathe. Calm breath relaxes the nervous system and calms the mind, leaving you in a much healthier state to face your fears.

To find out more about Sophie's talks, workshops, and writings, go to sophiesabbage.com. Rachel shares her expertise on well-being on her blog, towardswellbeing.wordpress.com.

SET FORWARD

How you think and feel about your intelligence and ability is often decided in childhood and can appear fixed, but with self-awareness and determination you have the power to adjust this perception and change the course of your life

Do you believe that your intelligence, your character, and your creativity is set, that they can't be altered, and that failure is best avoided? Or do you think that failure is an opportunity to grow and develop? On the surface, they're straightforward questions but your answer has an impact on how you live your life, and has done since you were a child.

How you respond to these statements indicates whether you have a fixed or growth mindset. Carol Dweck, Stanford University psychologist and a leading authority on the subject of mindset traits, describes a fixed mindset as having a certain personality and character and a view that these can't be altered. Such a person feels driven to prove and guard their set abilities at all times. With a fixed mindset, failure is a setback, it means you're not smart

or talented and you're not fulfilling your potential. Effort shouldn't be required because if you're clever or have a talent you shouldn't need to try hard.

With a growth mindset, however, your basic qualities can be developed and grown by effort, experience, and help from other people. Failure is seen as a chance to learn and grow as well as an opportunity to increase your intelligence. If you put in the effort, if you persist and learn from others, you can develop from where you started.

Mindset doesn't relate to your level of self-esteem or your levels of optimism. But the mindset you adopt from an early age does affect all areas of your life, including your behavior, how you deal with success and failure in your personal and professional life, and your level of happiness.

When you're considering trying something new, pay attention to how you talk to yourself about it. Is the fixed mindset telling you that you don't want to look a fool? Or is the growth mindset telling you to try?

Childhood indicators

Professor Dweck has carried out many research studies over the years and which mindset you adopt can be clearly shown from when you're a young child. For the first part of your life you learn and develop by persisting and not giving up. Learning to walk takes time and perseverance, babies fall down many times but they get up and take another step and each time they do they learn and develop their ability to walk. But this way of thinking may change.

One study gave four year olds some easy jigsaws to piece together. After they finished the task, the children were given the choice of another easy jigsaw to tackle or a more difficult one. Those with a fixed mindset chose to stick with the easy jigsaws because they knew they'd be able to complete them and wanted to feel sure of their success. The children with a growth mindset opted for the harder puzzle and found the choice itself puzzling, wondering why they shouldn't want to be challenged.

At this young age the focus may be on jigsaws but as you get older the choices become bigger and they have a greater impact on your life. If the fixed mindset means you don't want to risk trying something and failing, you could turn down a wide range of opportunities. If you believe that either a person is creative or they're not—and you think you're not—there's no point in even trying to learn to knit or draw. But you could be missing out on the chance to learn a craft that could give you great enjoyment and in which you could become highly skilled.

Similarly, if you don't wish to risk rejection you may decide not to talk to a stranger on the other side of the room and possibly miss out on the chance of making a friend, finding a life partner, or even a new employer. If you're sure of your own intelligence and skills, and don't believe they can be developed or improved, you're limiting your potential to be better, to be more fulfilled and to increase the difference you can make in the world.

With a fixed mindset you're looking for validation, for approval. With a growth one there's a passion for learning, a belief that effort and practice will cultivate intelligence, creativity, and even relationships. Where someone with a fixed mindset might see themselves as failing, a person with a growth version is likely to perceive it as learning.

In her book, *Mindset: Changing The Way You Think To Fulfill Your Potential*, Professor Dweck writes: "In one world—the world of fixed traits—success is about proving you're smart or talented. Validating yourself. In the other— the world of changing qualities—it's about stretching yourself to learn something new. Developing yourself."

Wanting to prove your intelligence and ability, to avoid failure, to hide where you're lacking, and to protect self-esteem may not just harm yourself but also have a negative impact on those around you. Professor Dweck gives numerous examples of multimillion-dollar corporations that went bust because the leader's fixed mindset refused to adapt, take advice, or try new ways of working.

As the research study with four year olds demonstrated, a mindset is adopted early in life. It can be reinforced or challenged by the individual or those around them. When a child answers a math question correctly or produces a drawing you can respond by affirming their ability or their effort. You could tell them: "That's fantastic, you're so clever" or "That's fantastic, you tried really hard." While these statements differ by only a few words, their meaning and impact vary. By telling the child they're clever the speaker is praising their ability and sending them into the fixed mindset. In contrast, when the focus is on the child's effort they're directing them toward the growth mindset.

In another study by Professor Dweck and her colleagues, teenage students were given 10 problems from a nonverbal IQ test, most of them did very well and they were praised for their performance. Some students were told: "Wow, you got (X) many right. That's a really good score. You must be smart at this." And other students were told: "Wow, you got (X) many right. That's a really good score. You must have worked really hard." When the students were given a choice of trying a new challenging task, the teenagers whose ability was praised didn't want to have a go while almost all of the others who had their effort pointed out wanted to attempt the new challenge.

The students were then given a new set of problems where they didn't do as well. Those who had been directed into the fixed mindset by having their intelligence praised no longer thought they were smart—failing at the problems meant they weren't clever after all. The students whose efforts had been praised took their results as an indicator to try harder and apply new strategies.

Deceptive leanings

The most shocking finding of this particular study was that the fixed mindset encouraged dishonesty. The students were asked to write letters to their peers describing the experience and their test scores. Forty percent of the ability-praised, fixed mindset teenagers lied about their scores to make themselves sound more successful. Says Professor Dweck: "In the fixed mindset, imperfections are shameful—especially if you're talented—

so they lied them away. What's so alarming is that we took ordinary children and made them into liars, simply by telling them they were smart."

It works for adults too. You may not often receive the kind of praise children get but you do talk to and criticize or praise yourself. When you're considering doing something new, whether it's going for a job interview, asking someone out on a date, joining a running club, or painting with watercolors, pay attention to how you talk to yourself about it. Is the fixed mindset telling you that you don't want to look a fool, that this isn't something you're good at and you shouldn't bother pursuing it any further? Or is the growth mindset telling you to try, that this could be the start of a new adventure, that it will be fun to learn and stretch yourself?

Or when you've taken that step, pushed yourself into your stretch zone only for things to not turn out as well as you hoped, what mindset are you adopting? Do you tell yourself that you should have known you'd fail, that it's not something you're capable of and you won't put yourself at risk again? Or can you look at it as a learning experience, think about what you can do to help yourself next time, consider what you might need to work on developing?

By now you probably have an idea of which mindset you've favored in your life. If it's the growth mindset this article may have been something of a revelation as you didn't realize that others could think with a fixed mindset. And if yours is a fixed mindset there's good news, it doesn't need to stay fixed. By moving your focus away from ability, judging, set intelligence, and seeing failure as permanent, and instead considering how you can grow and develop through effort, from others, and through learning from all your experiences, you can adopt a more growth-oriented mindset and open up to the opportunities all around you.

WORDS: GABRIELLE TREANOR. ILLUSTRATION: ANIESZKA BANKS

No more sorries

Being mindful about when and where to apologize matters more than you might imagine

Sorry is often a difficult word to say, especially when it comes after a tricky situation or event. Yet in everyday life, it's repeated time and again, for the tiniest things and for no real reason. You want to squeeze by someone blocking an aisle in the grocery store, so you say: "Sorry, could I get past please?"; you need to gain someone's attention and announce: "Sorry, can I just ask…" or you arrive early for a meeting, your colleague is already there, and you say: "I'm so sorry I kept you waiting." Sound familiar?

All these scenarios have in common an apology that isn't necessary. You've done nothing wrong and there's no need to make amends. It's perfectly reasonable to want to walk along a grocery store aisle, or to ask someone a question, so where's the need for an apology? You want to attract the person's attention in a polite and friendly manner, so "hello" or "excuse me" would suffice. Similarly, because a colleague decided to arrive extra early for a meeting, there's no need for you to behave as though you're running late.

So, why do people apologize unnecessarily, and does it matter? It matters because saying sorry isn't the same as saying hello or excuse me, which are neutral terms. Sorry is an apology. It's an admission that you're in the wrong. By using the word sorry, you aren't simply attracting a person's attention, you're apologizing for doing it and that's different. It suggests you're apologizing for speaking up.

Kick the habit

When someone apologizes the reciprocal response is to accept their apology and forgive them. So, in these everyday examples, what role does forgiveness have, what do you need to be forgiven for? For being in that place at that time? For being you?

Although you don't feel sorry for what you're saying or doing (and there's no reason why you should), the recipient could conclude that you do. One of the ways to present yourself to others is with language. By being mindful of words, you reduce the likelihood of being misunderstood and ensure you present the real you.

It can help to consider how "thank you" may be more appropriate. For example, you've had an exhausting day at work and you're venting to a friend about a challenging project. They've listened, offered sympathy, and been supportive. And so you apologize for complaining and being negative. Everyone has tough days where they need

to share how they feel. Is this a bad thing to do? Are you wrong to express how you feel? Is this a situation where you have something to apologize for?

Friends listen and give the support they can. When a friend helps you they don't do it expecting to be thanked, and they certainly don't expect an apology. Your appreciation is enough to make them feel glad they were able to be there for you. An apology, on the other hand, could make them feel as though they've failed to help you.

Imagine the post-exhausting day scene again, but this time swap the word sorry for the word thanks. So, after offloading about your awful day, you thank your friend for listening to you and for being supportive. How does that feel? You recognize you have a good friend and feel grateful you can share your emotions with someone who's on your side. And your listening friend is happy they were able to help. What shift can you sense in moving from a place of apology to a place of gratitude?

Another example is when you realize you've not replied to an email. You meant to respond immediately, but it slipped your mind and a few days have passed. You don't wish to appear rude by ignoring the fact the recipient may have been waiting for a reply. There are two options: apologize for being slow to reply or thank them for their patience. Both recognize the delay, but the former begins the conversation negatively, whereas the latter is positive.

There are many occasions where swapping the word sorry for thanks will change the dynamic of an interaction. Everyone has as much right as the next person to be heard and seen. You're allowed to feel what you're feeling, to express yourself, to take up space. You can still be kind, courteous, and compassionate to those around you.

You can attract someone's attention with a smile and a friendly hello or excuse me before making your request. Being the second person to arrive at a meeting doesn't make you late or in the wrong. You can thank a friend for listening, for their support, for being loyal. You can acknowledge another person's expectations with appreciation rather than apology.

There are times when a sincere apology, from the heart, is necessary—for when something wrong has been said or done. But there are many times when apologies aren't the best or even appropriate option. And that includes when you're being a thoughtful, considerate, caring person.

WORDS: GABRIELLE TREANOR. ILLUSTRATION: STEPHANIE HOFMANN

THE IMPOSTOR WITHIN

*Behind the façade of many a talented person lurks a conviction that they're a fake—
an inadequate, incompetent failure who's just lucked in and landed a great job—and
a fear that they'll soon be exposed. Impostor syndrome is real. And it's preventing too
many people from fulfilling their potential*

Fifteen years ago I was accepted onto a prestigious masters degree in creative writing at Glasgow University in Scotland. At a welcome lunch to get to know the other students and staff I discovered the institution had received 400 applications and I was one of 20 who had made the grade. I suddenly became gripped by the horrifying thought that there had been a mistake. What if the university had meant to accept someone else on the course but had somehow sent the letter to me instead?

As time went on this feeling faded. It was the nature of the course to give and receive constructive feedback and as fellow students commented favorably on my work my confidence grew. In time, I believed Glasgow had meant to choose me after all.

What is impostor syndrome?
For me, those nagging feelings of doubt faded, but what if they hadn't? Impostor syndrome is defined by Dr. Valerie Young, author of *The Secret Thoughts of Successful Women*, as being when "people have difficulty owning their accomplishments and dismiss them to factors outside of themselves such as luck, help from others, or an 'If I can do it, anybody can' attitude."

The term, impostor phenomenon, was coined in the 1970s by clinical psychologists, Drs. Suzanne Imes and Rose Clance. They conducted research with high-achieving women who nonetheless felt fraudulent, that somehow their academic or career successes were unwarranted. The pair concluded that the phenomenon was more common in women, or men with feminine qualities, although subsequent studies have suggested it may be just as common in men. The fact is around 80 percent of people will be affected by the syndrome at some point in their lives.

It can have devastating effects. Impostors feel terrified they will be found out and people will discover they're not as talented as they might appear. Many believe they are less able than their peers and need to make up for this by working extra hours. Alternatively, they fly under the radar and don't go for the job, promotion or career of their dreams because they don't feel they are good enough to do it. In meetings, they don't ask questions for fear they will be revealed as "stupid." But these hiding strategies can cause physical exhaustion, anxiety, and depression as life isn't lived to the full and the person feels their outward appearance of a talented, successful person is a façade.

Valerie says impostor syndrome is common in fields where people's work is openly criticized, for example, academic or creative disciplines. Actor Kate Winslet and musician Lady Gaga are said to experience the syndrome and late poet and civil rights campaigner Maya Angelou once said: "I have written 11 books and each time I think, 'Uh oh, they're going to find out now. I've run a game on everybody, and they're going to find me out.'"

How is it caused? Childhood can play a role. Valerie says children of perfectionist parents sometimes internalize a

sense of failure. This feeling is also shared by those whose achievements are ignored. Equally, being given too much praise can dilute a sense of achievement. But Valerie is quick to point out that the numbers of people affected indicate the causes are also found outside the home.

Alice Irving is a woman's coach who helps mid-career women to realize their full potential. She links the syndrome to the way Western society places value on what are traditionally perceived as masculine qualities—productivity, winning, and losing—while underestimating traits that are often regarded as feminine, such as collaboration and connection.

She pinpoints impostor syndrome as the sense that people aren't able to bring their whole authentic selves to the workplace and suggests this is behind the feeling of being a fraud. In a sense, some women feel they are putting on an act—even if they aren't fully conscious of it—in order to conform and fit in to a masculine society.

Knatokie Ford was accepted into Harvard to do a PhD in STEM (science, technology, engineering, and mathematics). She developed a new sense of style because she didn't want to be perceived as a "girly girl," but felt so intimidated by her environment that she left and took a job as a teacher. She worked in an underserved area of

LA and found that children there were already feeling insecure and "stupid" by seventh grade. The realization prompted her to return to Harvard and confront her impostor feelings. Today, she is a biomedical scientist with a PhD, served as a policy advisor at the White House during President Obama's term in office and is founder and CEO of Fly Sci Enterprise, an education and media consulting organization focused on leveraging the power of storytelling to promote social change, particularly in science, technology, engineering, and mathematics. She also just happens to love lipstick and big hair.

Are there steps impostors can take to appreciate their worth and talents? Comic-book author Neil Gaiman met Neil Armstrong at a night for scientists and writers. Amazingly, this legendary astronaut and aerospace engineer confided to Neil that he felt out of place at the event. It was this admission that helped the latter finally see the folly of his own impostor syndrome. The man who walked on the moon, whose achievements had been acknowledged the world over, still had impostor moments. Don't let yours hinder your progress or undermine your success.

EXPERT TIPS FOR OVERCOMING IMPOSTOR SYNDROME

1 Drop unrealistic expectations of yourself
Valerie says impostors tend to be perfectionists who struggle if they make mistakes. A big difference between an impostor and nonimpostor is the latter can put mistakes into context whereas an impostor feels great shame. Acknowledge it's okay to make mistakes. It doesn't lessen your talent or ability. It just means you're human.

2 Think different thoughts
"There's only one difference between impostors and nonimpostors and that's their thoughts," says Valerie. Try to pay conscious attention to your thoughts when having an impostor moment. What standard and expectation are you holding yourself to overtly or covertly? "I should have…" or "if I was really intelligent, capable, and confident then I would know all the answers," or "I wouldn't have made that mistake if I knew what I was doing," or "I shouldn't have needed any help." Try to reframe your thoughts to think like a nonimpostor.

3 Bring presence to the situation
Amy Cuddy, author of *Presence; Bringing Your Boldest Self to Your Biggest Challenges*, says when you unite your body and mind, you can be your true authentic self. She defines presence as "when you are attuned to and are comfortably able to access and express—your best qualities, your boldest self, your core values, your skills, your knowledge, and your personality." She points out that it's about responding to what is actually happening in a situation rather than what you fear is happening. She recommends power poses, for example, standing hands outstretched, up in the air, or hands on hips in something of a Wonder Woman impersonation. These poses help to boost testosterone, lower cortisol, and help to encourage confidence in the natural, talented self.

4 Get to know your authentic self
Alice recommends starting an inner-dialogue with your authentic self so that you can practice showing up as your whole true person, rather than just the parts you perceive others will find acceptable.

She teaches women how to practice self-care, which is more than just going to bed early or buying a nice dress. "The beginnings of solid self-care are much more subtle than that," she says. What impostors need to do is notice, moment by moment, "What would feel good for me right now?"; "What would be nice for me right now?"; "How can I be kind to myself for the next minute?"; "What would be a great way for me to spend this last free half hour of my day?" By listening to your authentic needs and desires you can move away from acting out of the fear of failure, or being found out.

Part of the solution is also to understand boundaries. This helps when it's necessary to say no to a request—rather than saying yes to everything because you think it's a necessary part of your façade.

5 Testimonial therapy
Ask clients, colleagues, and friends for written feedback and spend time reading it. Allow it to sink in so you can start to feel your self-worth. "It's all about being welcome in the world," says Alice, "and you can live your dreams, and be secure in your own individual gifts and talents, and what you have to contribute."

The guilt complex

Face up to your wrongdoing, however big or small, and seek forgiveness

When I was a little girl I'd spend hours in the fields and woods, seeking out a magical world of butterflies hiding in the grass. One day, a friend and I were playing at a spot that was always favored by a kaleidoscope of butterflies when we came across a big beautiful creature that had died. We were excited by the opportunity to marvel at the delicacy of her wings up close and study the complex colors that seemed to change with the light. There was also a thrill that we could take her home with us as a keepsake. But we both wanted the butterfly, each claiming to have "found it first." To settle the predicament, my friend managed to catch another and squeezed it hard enough to ensure we both went home with our own butterfly.

It wasn't the crime of the century, nor has it plagued me in subsequent years, yet it was my first real feeling of guilt and I can remember it as if it was yesterday. I recall my mom coming to collect me and asking: "Where did you get those?" My reply? "We found them." The lie jarred, it was hollow. There was almost a feeling of tightness in my throat and emptiness in my cheat. All the joy we felt, marveling at the beauty of the creature, had disappeared and I sat in silence on the drive home, my butterfly

wrapped in tissue paper on my lap. When we arrived back I burst into tears and confessed everything to my mom.

I hold the belief that most people are doing the best with what they know, the tools, conditioning, and knowledge that they find themselves with in each moment. Yet sometimes, on occasion, it seems to go wrong. What follows such errors of judgment is a hollow feeling, much like the anguish I experienced with my childhood butterfly.

If you have ever let others down (we are all only human, after all) you might know how this feels. The misdemeanor could have been anything—a dishonest answer to a partner; bumping into a neighbor's car and quickly driving away unseen; claiming to be busy at work when a friend asks for help. The result is a feeling of guilt.

When the complexities of this emotion are considered, however, it's possible to see it can sometimes be useful. It allows you to become clear on your core values and to make choices in the future that match more closely your personality. It's important, though, not to beat yourself up about it and not to let it fester.

My friend and I made a mistake and I still remember the feeling of guilt, but to err is human.

When your actions or behavior—knowingly or unknowingly—cause hurt, how do you get over the feeling of guilt to ensure one mistake doesn't do even more harm? How do you cultivate a healthy relationship with this complicated emotion? Here are five suggestions…

1 Face what you've done

If you've dinged your neighbor's car and didn't confess you might inflict a sense of guilt upon yourself. You have a choice—face what you've done or don't. Being honest may result in consequences for you and them, but ask yourself, in the moment, what's the right thing to do?

Guilt can then serve a relatively functional purpose. It can act as an internal warning system within the wiring of your nervous system which helps you identify unethical behavior and then choose a course of action from that moment. Perhaps it's as simple as an unconditional apology, a confession or a chance to right any wrongs. Face it rather than allowing it to fester.

2 Explore the feeling

According to Anxiety Care UK "guilt is rooted in low self-esteem." It might be helpful to ask yourself why you're holding on to guilt? Could it perhaps be as a noble gesture? You've done something wrong and you won't forgive yourself as a declaration of your remorse? This might do more harm than good. Research suggests this is not an efficient way to help you to act better, or to make better choices in the future. "Study after study shows that self-criticism is consistently associated with less motivation and worse self-control," reports Anxiety Care UK. "It is the single biggest predictor for depression."

And a festering feeling of guilt won't help you make nobler choices in the future.

3 Be clear on your values

See any guilt you feel as a result of your actions as a warning light for your moral code. What personal value of yours did you break for this feeling of guilt to surface? This understanding can be used as a tool to ensure your decisions, actions, words, or gestures are aligned to what is truly an expression of you. Spend time exploring this either through writing a journal, meditation, or seeking out support.

4 Be present

Mindfulness is the deliberate practice of being present in the moment, on purpose, without judgment. This can become a significant and useful tool in overcoming feelings of guilt or shame and help you to choose more wisely in the future. Being deliberately present in the moment is a freedom from the past. It offers a clean slate to take action from, to let go of, and to move forward without the burden of guilt.

The practice of mindfulness when applied to action means that you evaluate what needs to happen on facts and what's real in the moment. This can help to make more ethical, loving, and wise choices rather than ones based on past guilt, false realities, or future worries.

"Forgiving yourself requires honesty and self-acceptance," says clinical psychologist Diane Cottesloe. "Clearing away the veil of guilt allows us to be more connected to what it is that we are experiencing, our thoughts, and our actions in light of that experience and, thus, to be more present with our experience, our emotions, and ourselves.'

5 Seek forgiveness

No one can change the past, but by practicing being in the present, taking responsibility, and facing the root cause of the feeling of guilt, there is personal power to change the future.

There is a beautiful Hawaiian ritual called ho'oponopono that is practiced as a form of reconciliation and forgiveness. The literal translation is: "To put to right; to put in order or shape, correct, revise, adjust, amend, regulate, arrange, rectify, tidy up, make orderly or neat." Within relationships, family units, or community groups, an individual will recite: "I'm sorry. Please forgive me. Thank you. I love you," in a ceremony, taking responsibility and asking for reconciliation.

Ho'oponopono, according to author and speaker Joe Vital, is a ritual to admit that "we are all responsible for everything that we see in our world. By taking full personal responsibility and then healing the wounded places within ourselves, we can literally heal ourselves and our world."

Therefore, use feelings of guilt as an opportunity for learning, as an opportunity of reconciliation, and to take responsibility for yourself. It's true that when you forgive or confess it doesn't change the past, but it might just change the future.

WORDS: JOANNA HULIN. ILLUSTRATIONS: STEPHANIE HOFMANN

People like *you*

The desire to be liked runs deep, but if you find yourself subjugating your own needs and opinions for fear of losing the approval of friends and colleagues, then the chances are yours is coming at too high a price. Do you have the disease to please?

Helpful, always available, willing to change plans at the drop of a hat. At first glance, they're all positive attributes. But take another look and put them in a different context—one where they form part of an acute and uncontrolled desire to please. Now they have the potential to be damaging, especially if they're tied to a need for approval, anxiety about other people's opinions, and a desire always to be liked.

Many people worry about what others think of them and fear disapproval, disappointment, or judgment. It's as though their own opinions, values, knowledge, and experiences are less important than gaining other people's approval. When this craving becomes too great, when the disease to please takes over, they tailor their lives (and themselves) to fit others' expectations.

Are you a people pleaser?
If you're a people pleaser, you probably put more effort into assuring other people's happiness than you do your own. You may try your hardest to keep everyone around you happy, even changing your behavior to please them, agreeing to do things you don't want to do, or subjugating your own needs and wants to avoid disapproval or retribution. Then, even when you feel upset, taken advantage of, or resentful, you insist that everything is fine.

Say, for example, you're struggling with an assertive family member who regularly turns up at your home and demands you babysit their children while they go to the gym. You have work and chores to do but rather than disappoint this person you agree to look after the kids.

As a result, you're left feeling exhausted, and mention to a friend that you think this person is taking advantage of your caring nature. "Why don't you just tell them how you feel?" is their advice. "I can't do that. What if they get upset or don't like me any more?"

The need for external approval by another person—no matter how unreasonable they're being—becomes more important than the need to look after your own personal and emotional well-being.

The disease to please can also result in people remaining in unhealthy relationships because they continually focus on the need to ensure a partner's happiness and to gain their approval even when it's at the cost of personal development and goals. Healthy compromise is one thing, sacrificing what really matters to you is another.

If this sounds like you, try asking yourself these questions. A journal can be a constructive way of exploring if you are placing too great an importance on other people's approval of you. You could write down your answers and then come back to them in a day or two.

- *Are you trying too hard to be liked by everyone else?*
- *Do you think it's possible for everyone to like you?*
- *In what situations and with whom do you find yourself displaying people-pleasing behavior?*
- *How regularly do you stop yourself from doing or saying something out of fear that someone won't like you or that you may offend them?*

It's time to approve of yourself

When you seek appreciation from others, be it a boss, partner, family member, or complete stranger, you are looking for a fix of approval to feel good about yourself. But no amount of appreciation from others is ever going to be enough to make you happy.

Even worse, when you don't get your fix, you may turn against yourself, feeling as though you've done something wrong or that you're a bad person. This can leave you feeling low and send you back to seeking approval. Before you know it you're stuck in an addictive cycle.

The key to breaking free is to begin to gently give yourself the approval and internal validation that you crave. When you learn to be happy and content with who you are it's empowering—and easier to stop being so concerned about what other people think of you.

It is better to be yourself and risk having people not like you than to suffer the stress and tension that comes from pretending to be someone you're not, or professing to like something that you don't. Give yourself the freedom to approve of yourself.

Start by treating yourself with love and compassion and approve of your own life—even if other people don't. Give up expecting other people to understand or approve of you, it isn't their life and they haven't shared your experiences.

Remember, nobody has exactly the same goals, beliefs, or desires, so expecting other people to understand you in the same way that you do really is a thankless task. Learn to tune into and honor your own choices, and don't doubt yourself just because someone else doesn't get it.

Make peace that not everyone in the world is going to like you and start being your own best friend and advocate, rather than your own worst enemy.

You deserve to live your life based on your own personal preferences, caring about your needs. Thinking of others is one thing, but pleasing others is not the same as *helping* others. Learn to love yourself.

"When you're different, sometimes you don't see all the people who accept you for what you are. All you notice is the person who doesn't"

JODI PICOULT

TIPS FOR RELEASING PEOPLE-PLEASING BEHAVIOR

- If you recognize yourself as a people pleaser, acknowledge that you can do something about it. It may be difficult at first, but it will leave you empowered in the long run.
- If you worry about being judged, remind yourself how likely it is that people are not even thinking about you. Try to keep things in context. People will think what they want to think anyway.
- Get clear on your own priorities in life. What is important to you? How do you wish to spend your time? Remember, you have the right to decide what to do, who to spend time with, and to fulfill your own needs.
- Remind yourself that you always have a choice to say no. If someone asks for your help, consider the impact it will have on your time and energy. Recognize you're in complete control of how you spend your time and who you spend it with.
- If saying yes to everything has become a habit, try something new. Say: "I'll think about that and get back to you." Then give yourself time to consider.

Stick with it

Bear in mind that when you first free yourself of the disease to please, there may be a period of adjustment. Emotions such as guilt or fear may rise to the surface and tempt you to revert to old behaviors. It's important to acknowledge these uncomfortable feelings, but also to give yourself credit for what you have achieved and let go of any angst. Remind yourself that embedding new habits can take time, but it will be worth it. You'll be truly you and the people who really matter will like and love you just as much as ever.

WORDS: LISA PHILLIPS, AMAZINGCOACHING.CO.UK. ILLUSTRATION: STEPHANIE HOFMANN

Quick to judge?

It's all too easy to make snap assessments, but often they reveal more about you than the other person. Let go of judgment and you might take hold of a whole new world

Are you a judgmental person? Do you find yourself thinking negative thoughts or gossiping about others? Many dictionaries define judgment as "the ability to make considered decisions or come to sensible conclusions." But it's also explained as "an opinion or conclusion," and this is where many judgments miss the mark. So, you may think that you're doing the former, and being considered, but if you look just that little more closely, a lot of the thoughts that flit constantly across your mind are your opinion.

The quick fix
Judgment is like fast food. Making a negative appraisal about another person is like a quick fix that makes you feel better. You look at a person society perceives to be overweight eating chocolate and feel better about your own size. Or you think negatively about a colleague who spends time on Facebook and convince yourself you're a far more diligent employee. But what's really going on when you leap to these conclusions?

Gabrielle Bernstein is an author, speaker, and self-proclaimed "spirit junkie." In her book, *Judgement Detox*, she reveals how judgment says more about you than the person you're judging, and that it's sometimes because they reopen deep wounds.

For example, a friend has a successful job and you criticize her for not spending enough time with her family. The reality might be that she's juggling the situation as best as she can and she thinks deeply about how to ensure she balances work with family life. It could be that your assessment of the situation comes from personal insecurity about your career achievements.

The reasons for making such assessments can have long, deep roots into the past. Someone who had weight concerns as a child may think badly of others they consider to be chubby while a person who was constantly chastised in childhood for being lazy might externalize this in their perception of a colleague as work-shy because

they scan Facebook every couple of hours. Gabrielle insists that judgment is used as a defense mechanism. Another person triggers your "stuff" and the response is like a Band-Aid placed on the wound. This helps you feel better in the moment, without looking at what's actually going on beneath the surface. Everyone does it. Challenges and difficulties encountered in childhood can make people vulnerable and there isn't always a safe space to explore and heal wounds when we reach adulthood.

When I read *Judgement Detox*, I was shocked. I like to think of myself as an empathetic human being who can see the good in everyone. I started, however, to notice my judgments and saw that they were almost like an involuntary reflex. They happened quickly, before I could stop them. It was like I was constantly trying to make myself feel better by assessing people on the street, acquaintances, or even friends and loved ones. I judged the woman who was too self-absorbed to think

'Judgment is the number-one reason we feel blocked, sad and alone'

GABRIELLE BERNSTEIN

to hold the door open for me as I followed her into a store; the boy walking up the middle of the street staring at his phone and not looking where he was going; the acquaintance who talked about herself all of the time and never asked how I was doing.

If I had only stopped to think a little longer, I might have considered these appraisals to be incorrect. What if the didn't-keep-the-door-open woman was stressed after hearing bad news about a family member?; what if the phone-fixated boy was anxious about a girl not responding to his messages?; what if my acquaintance was impossibly nervous about an upcoming job interview and couldn't see beyond it? It could be that I was missing a significant part of the story.

You could leave judgments unaddressed. After all, if you don't voice them, what harm are you doing? Gabrielle says this approach ignores the core wounds and can also result in loneliness and isolation. Instead of seeing what common ground there might be with another person and how you might get along, you separate and disconnect. "Judgment is the number-one reason we feel blocked, sad, and alone," says Gabrielle.

She adds that our true nature is love—a Buddha-like spirit. Those who judge are separating themselves from their true nature. Like me, there are many people who are unaware of how much they do this, and how it eats away at their well-being. Pay conscious attention to this behavior—it can be eye-opening.

Judgment day

Spend a day noticing the assessments you make, but don't criticize yourself for any negative thoughts. Gabrielle recommends that you "witness the judgment without judgment." It's important to remember there's nothing wrong with you for coming to false conclusions. They are reflections of ways you may have been hurt and difficulties you may have faced. Be kind to yourself and give yourself the same compassion you would a friend. This is a positive step to becoming conscious of your thought processes and, in time, it will allow you to let go.

By observing the judgment, you can separate yourself from it. In that moment of attention, you are the part of yourself that notices rather than gets caught up in the thought. Focus on how you feel in and after the moment. Do you get a quick buzz of superiority that quickly fades? You might want to write down each judgment you make, so that you can reflect on them at the end of the day. Ask yourself if there is a core wound or difficulty in your own life that might be behind the judgment.

This is an emotional and intense process that demands honesty as you admit to yourself that your thoughts about others may say more about you than the reality of the situation. Gabrielle describes an emotional freedom technique (also known as tapping) that helps to release the feelings and trauma that cause people to make certain judgments. Journaling is useful to process feelings, but always try to end on a positive note: Think about what you learned from the situation, what you gained in terms of personal growth, and what you hope for in the future. If things get overwhelming, talking things over with a doctor or counsellor can also help.

Cultivate compassion

According to Gabrielle, love and compassion are the opposite of judgment. She recommends a beautiful practice where you spend an entire week focusing on the light in other people. To do this, repeat: "The light in you is all I see" each time you come across someone. Gabrielle says: "If you are spending all your time focusing on people's light, you have no time to judge."

You may find people reacting differently to you as they sense your positive energy. After a while, you may begin to feel a deep sense of well-being and joy.

Other ways you could consider to cultivate compassion could include the Buddhist loving-kindness meditation, which focuses on sending loving feelings to others, as explained by one of America's leading spiritual teachers Sharon Salzberg in her book *Loving-Kindness: The Revolutionary Art of Happiness*. Gabrielle also describes tailor-made meditations to help release judgments.

WORDS: KATE ORSON. ILLUSTRATIONS: ANIESZKA BANKS

Listen to people's stories

I once worked as an English tutor in Asia and one of my students, a 14-year-old boy, complained about climbing the flights of stairs to my apartment. I found myself thinking how lazy he was to be grumbling about walking until I discovered he had a problem with one of his legs.

Experiences like this have taught me that there's always a reason behind a person's actions, and the more we take time to listen to each other's stories, the more a person's behavior makes sense. The real trick is to dig that little bit deeper and truly pause to listen, before deciding if any snap assessments you might have made are correct.

Distinguish between judgment and discernment

Gabrielle makes an important distinction between judgment and discernment. As you start to notice the snap appraisals you make about others, you should not discount intuitive or thoughtful conclusions, or discernment. She says that one way to tell the difference between judgment and discernment is to notice how you feel. If you feel bad, then you're most likely judging the other person. "When you make a decision that feels good and flows from your authentic truth, you know it's not back with the ego's judgment."

These practices are not intended to make you a completely nonjudgmental person. Rather, they allow you to choose not to believe your assessments any more. As you spend time paying mindful attention to your thoughts, you can let go of your judgmental self and identify with your loving self instead. It may be hard at times for your ego to let go of the stories it has told you, but a new world will unfold. Instead of judgment and disconnection, you can see other people's light, and as a result, you can focus on connection and joy.

Keeping the peace

Maybe you're sitting at the dinner table while a family member advocates a course of action you feel to be unwise, or you've waxed lyrical about a political passion of yours to a colleague only to realize they hold a completely different opinion on the subject. What tends to be your default mechanism? Do you make a hasty retreat from the choppy conversational waters or dive in and tackle them head on? Those who are conflict-avoidant might tend to opt for the former only to be left with a niggling feeling that they didn't argue their case and do justice to their views. Others happily voice their opinions—loudly—convinced they're right and a companion can and even, perhaps, should, be persuaded to change their beliefs. It's difficult to find the middle ground. So, what can you do? Here are a few tips on how to navigate tricky situations without firing any shots and with everyone's integrity kept intact.

1 Embrace your wrongness

Humans tend to think they're logical creatures. They like to be right and often assume that they've used good judgment to come to their conclusions. Researchers have found, however, that people's decision-making process may not be so logical after all. Antonio Damasio, neuroscientist and author of *The Strange Order of Things*, found that patients who had damaged the part of the brain where emotions are processed struggled to make decisions.

This suggests that emotions play a role in the stance you take in an argument. It's also been found that people operate according to a confirmation bias. They have a tendency to favor information that confirms their beliefs and disfavor evidence that contradicts them.

Kathryn Schulz is the author of *Being Wrong: Adventures in The Margin of Error*. She explains that it's the nature of the human mind to make things up, to be imaginative and creative, and that for this reason being wrong is part of the fundamental human condition.

Kathryn points out that people are brought up to place great importance on being right. Their entire school life is often based on getting good grades and their career is about not failing. This can lead people to feel a desperate need to be right, and when they are faced with someone who has a different opinion, they might also feel a need to change their mind.

Kathryn says: "It's possible to step outside the feeling of being right and, if you do so, it's the single greatest moral intellectual and creative leap you can make. When you are open to the possibility that you might be wrong, you can be more flexible and more open to listening to other people's opinions, even though you may not agree with them. Who really knows which of you is 'wrong' anyway? Perhaps it's even both of you."

2 Check in with your own sense of peace

When you feel passionate about something you may harbor a desire to change someone's opinion. This can seem aggressive or argumentative, especially if you get caught up in a heated discussion. You may even feel angry that they can hold an opinion that to you may seem "ignorant" or "selfish."

Opening your mind to the possibility that you might be wrong allows you to let go of any urgency to persuade people to agree with your point of view. This can help you to approach conversations from a more peaceful place. Counsellor Shani Graves recommends that you are careful of your tone of voice and speak calmly from a place of understanding and empathy for the other person, even if you disagree with their views. Try to keep in mind: "It's not what you say, but how you say it."

Bianca L. Rodriguez, a psychotherapist and breathwork teacher, advises that a cool mindset helps: "If you have a lot of energy around a topic, I recommend journaling, meditating, or going for a walk outside beforehand, so that you can speak from a place of calmness. This will allow you to express yourself clearly and navigate the discussion from your heart."

3 Listen and give your full attention

What people want more than anything is to be listened to. "Being heard is so close to being loved that for the average person, they're almost indistinguishable," says David Augsburger, author of *The Love of Letting Be*. Sometimes people get caught up in a row because they want the other person to listen to them. Instead, they might want to practice listening.

Give the other person your warm attention. Try to let go of your feelings and focus on this moment of human connection. Take a deep breath and let the other person express their thoughts. Being able to talk freely allows them to release some of the heat from their argument and once they've had a chance to air their view, they may be more receptive to your thoughts and be more inclined to replicate your helpful listening skills.

While you're listening, attempt to focus on what is positive about the conversation and the other person's point of view. Marriage therapists John and Julie Gottman found that healthy marriages had five times as many positive interactions as negative ones. So if you feel like a conversation is descending into the negative, focus on saying something to let the listener know you like and respect them and are interested in what they are saying. Just a few simple changes in the way you interact can make the world of difference.

4 When to speak up

As you approach your conversations more mindfully you may find there are times when you have something important to say and wonder about the most tactful, diplomatic way to say it. Many commentators, including Bianca, feel dissenting voices can be helpful. "We need more people to speak up in today's political climate in order to foster change," she says. But overtly trying to affect people's minds may be doomed to failure. Research suggests that when people hold strong beliefs they are even more likely to stand by them when they are presented with evidence that is contradictory to their opinions.

Bianca recommends that you start by asking yourself what your intention is and if it is to serve the greater good, then you should speak up. She suggests that you use "I" statements and be careful not to blame the other party as this will foster defensiveness. An "I" statement is nonconfrontational but direct. For example: "I believe/think/feel that there should be equality between men and women." They also help the other person to connect to you as a human being, making it more likely that they will understand your point of view.

5 Use stories instead of logic

Have you noticed how two sides in a debate often want the same thing at heart? For example, many politicians go into public life wanting to make the world a better place, but disagree on how to get there. Most parents want their kids to grow up happy and healthy but often have differing views on how to bring up a family. When you focus on what you have in common, you can build bridges.

In her memoir *A Land Twice Promised: An Israeli Woman's Quest for Peace*, Israeli author Noa Baum tells how an encounter with "the enemy"—a Palestinian woman she met in the US—helped her to understand the transformative power of stories for peace. "We were able to hold onto our compassion and talk in spite of differences because we were sharing our stories," she recalls. Today she works to use storytelling as a peace-building tool to overcome the fear of otherness. Noa believes the approach "creates an immediate sense of trust and intimacy. It allows us to suspend judgment and open up to different points of view without becoming defensive, and it facilitates and deepens our compassion." Storytelling, says Noa, allows people to consider information they might otherwise ignore.

Next time you want to put forward a particular point of view, try telling the story of why you hold this opinion. The listener might not change their mind, but hopefully they'll come to understand the reasons behind your thinking. And sharing stories may even bring you closer together.

Hop back to school

Artificial divisions between creativity and security are sometimes set in the classroom and continue through adulthood. By going back in time and unschooling your mind, you may chance upon a passion that invites a little risk but could bring a lot of personal fulfilment

Do you wish you could be more creative? Would you like to find work that you're passionate about? Most people have dreams, but sometimes it can be difficult to know where to start to achieve them. At school, you study and take exams, often with a focus on achieving good grades and going on to build a rewarding career. It can sometimes seem that there is little freedom to choose. As adults, this can cause conflict between seeking security and material success and taking a leap into the unknown by doing what you love.

Unschooling is a philosophy for teaching children. It is based on the idea that infants and young people can learn by following what brings them joy. The term was coined in the 1970s by John Holt, an American educator and author, who became disillusioned with the school system. He believed that given a rich learning environment children would naturally teach themselves when they were ready.

Unschooling is all about life-long learning and following what brings you joy. And the process is as applicable to adults as it is to children. It can help to reignite self-motivation to learn and to rediscover your passion. It can be difficult to know where to start, though, so here are a few tips on how to unschool your mind as an adult. You could talk through the ideas with a friend, analyse them in a journal or explore them in drawings.

Take a rest
A decade (at least) in the school system, time at university or an apprenticeship, followed by full-time work—in Western culture everything in life seems scheduled with little downtime. Yet the idea of taking time off can be scary. It may mean that you start to feel your emotions rather than being constantly too busy to pay them heed. There can also be guilt about doing nothing—surely being busy and productive is the right thing to do.

It can appear that if you spend a day watching a TV series on Netflix or taking a long luxurious bath that nothing much is happening. But as your body and mind are restored you may begin to notice different things, perhaps a spark of an idea or a memory of something you used to love. Rather than striving to achieve a target, you can wait and see what arises.

Follow the joy
Some children are born with a fierce stubborness. They know what they love to do and, given enough emotional safety to express themselves, they will strongly object if you try to recommend they do something else.

But children don't always have freedom of choice. The school system doesn't usually allow them to say 'no'. It could be argued that education trains young people to comply with the system's expectations and this can often lead them to lose touch with their inner 'yes'. This can be compounded by the responsibilities that come with adulthood. Everyone needs to deal with the practicalities of life and work to earn a living. Unfortunately, this often doesn't leave space to discover what will bring you joy and to say 'yes'. It could be that you might not even remember the passions you so loved in childhood.

Journalling can be a powerful way of getting in touch with what you love and figuring out ways to make time for it. First, write a list where you brainstorm as many things as possible that bring you joy. It could be anything from that first cup of tea in the morning to walking in nature. Next, ask yourself if there's anything else that you'd like to add to the list that you've never tried before. Trust your intuition and write down whatever answers pop into your head. Finally, take a look at what's holding you back from spending more time doing what you love and explore how you can bring more joy into your life.

How to say "yes"

1 Listen to your body

Many of life's difficulties happen when body and mind are in conflict with each other. On a Monday morning when the alarm goes off, your body might feel like spending another hour in bed but your mind knows it's time to get up. Maybe it's a Friday night and you're torn between partying with friends or having a relaxing night at home on the couch. Developing the art of listening to your body can help you to discover your joy and passion because you get in tune with what you really want. Yoga and meditation can help to deepen awareness and body sensitivity or you could try asking yourself the question: "What does my body need right now?" A walk in the park or a rest relaxing with a cup of coffee? In her book, *The Molecules of Emotion*, Dr. Candace Pert explains how the body is the unconscious mind where emotions are stored. By getting in touch with your body you get beyond the "I should" and gain access to your deep inner knowing of what you want to do.

2 Reflect on childhood and schooling

In *The Element: How Finding Your Passion Changes Everything*, Ken Robinson tells the story of a young girl in the 1930s who couldn't concentrate at school and was known as "wiggle bottom." The British author, speaker, and international advisor on education points out that in today's society the child would probably be tested for attention deficit hyperactivity disorder (ADHD), but this condition—and its diagnosis—wasn't readily available at the time. Instead, the girl and her mother went to a psychologist, who turned on the radio before the two adults left the room. While they were gone the girl danced to the music. The psychologist told her mother that there was nothing wrong with her daughter, that she was a dancer. The girl went on to become a professional ballerina. This is not to comment on ADHD, but to illustrate that there is value in exploring your own schooling experiences.

What did you like? And what was less appealing? What did you love doing as a child? Stuart Brown, founder of the National Institute for Play in California, explains that when you observe a child in free play that is completely undirected by adults you can often see clues as to what they will do for a living in their adult years. Are there moments and memories from childhood that might hold the key to your passion? And were there times you found you didn't like a subject? Might it have been because of the way it was taught?

3 Explore your inner voice

As you grow up, it's easy to internalize assumptions about the world and start to believe them as if they were your own. Who told you that you could never get rich doing what you love? Who said that giving up your job to travel the world was reckless? Discovering the origin of these voices and exploring how you feel about them can provide the key to breaking free and allow you to listen and pay heed to your own inner voice instead. Stand up to the voices and write down your responses.

4 Go on an artist's date

The Artist's Way by teacher Julia Cameron is a classic book for getting in touch with your creativity by free writing. She recommends taking yourself on a solo artist's date each week to explore a subject you find interesting—these are described as being "assigned play." They don't have to be overly artistic, but more about thinking about what you

WORDS: KATE ORSON. ILLUSTRATIONS: FRANCESCA-IANNACCONE

would find fun. It could be cloud watching, writing a letter to the person you'd like to be in five years' time, visiting a nearby town, or taking a new course at your local adult education center—it's entirely up to you.

5 Visualize your dream life

After exploring your creativity and what you love, try visualizing your future. Imagine where you will be in 10 years and write down the details. Where will you live? What will your job be? Hal Hershfield, assistant professor of marketing at UCLA Anderson School of Management, has found imagining your future self helps you to work toward making choices that will get you closer to reaching your goals.

6 Face your fears

You might want to ask yourself what you are afraid of? There may be an element of risk to following your path, but equally if you explore all the options there will most likely be steps that can make your goal feel more manageable. Go on, take the leap.

Embrace the (positive) messages

Changing negative thought patterns to positive ones can significantly improve happiness and well-being, but it isn't always easy. That's where encouraging affirmations and uplifting quotations can lend a hand

When my long-term relationship came to an end at the start of the year, the first thing a close friend suggested was following a stream of positivity accounts on Instagram. At first, I cringed at the cliché, but soon found myself saving quote after quote to my camera roll. In moments of despair, I found my bank of encouraging messages a great comfort—and I realized I wasn't the only one with this habit. I heard many tales of people using positivity quotes to help change their mindset.

Positive thought patterns
Psychotherapist Uxshely Chotai explains why engaging with positive thought can be influential. "Positive affirmations make us more aware of our thought processes and encourage self-compassion, which can help us retrain [our] inner dialogue," she says. Even better, the more you work on improving happiness levels, the more positive you become. Positivity breeds positivity.

Psychiatrist Arghya Sarkhel elaborates: "The brain can be conceptualized as a network of complex electrical wirings. Studies have shown how these circuits can be dampened when negative thinking becomes a default mode, while encouraging comments and affirmations that bring about positive experiences can help to strengthen these networks instead." This is partly because of the Reticular Activating System (RAS) at the base of the brain. Like a filter to the mind, the RAS processes data gained via the senses and helps prioritize what's important at that moment. "The more we engage in positive experiences and thought, the more we are activating our RAS to create a pattern where we prioritize information with positive qualities," says Arghya.

In other words, the more positivity that surrounds people, the more their ability to appreciate it improves. "This can be described as the 'therapeutic vicious cycle,'" says Arghya. "As RAS is connected with the circuits in our brain that relate to mood in the cortex, it helps to activate these circuits. We then tend to look out for similar experiences and the 'therapeutic cycle' continues." While the science makes sense, deciding to be—and remain-positive can be tough. What's easier is learning techniques that you can incorporate into daily life.

Practicing positivity
Nadia Narain, co-author of *Self-Care for The Real World: Practical Self-care Advice for Everyday*, says the first step to embracing more positive thought patterns is to notice how you think in certain situations. "What do you think when you look in the mirror? Do you focus on what's wrong with your face and body and let those bad thoughts fill you up, or do you simply notice? Once you become aware of what you are thinking you start to change those thoughts. In this case, thinking all the positives about your body."

For the second step, Nadia suggests changing the language you use when talking to yourself. "Try to have a different conversation with yourself. Instead of using phrases like 'I never' or 'I can't,' reframe it by using words like 'I'm willing to' or 'I will try.'"

If you find this difficult, that's when affirmations and quotes can be so useful. They give you something specific to focus on and provide a structured way to include positivity in your day. Nadia suggests putting them in places where you'll see them regularly, such as on the refrigerator or on a dressing table, or uploading them as a background to your phone. "Positive thinking is a constant work in progress and it takes time to find what works for you. But working on it can have such an amazingly wide effect on your well-being," adds Nadia.

Navigating the negative
While incorporating positivity into your day is important, learning to deal with the negative is also crucial. Trying to avoid negative thoughts altogether might be setting yourself up for failure. As Uxshely says, learning to know how to deal with these thoughts is key: "It's empowering to realize that we create our own experience of the world by the thoughts that we have."

The first step in letting go of negative thoughts is accepting that they come and go. "Once you have self-awareness and notice that you are experiencing a negative thought, you realize that it is just a thought and not reality," says Uxshely. "Often, negative thought patterns cycle because we believe them to be true, but a thought is only a thought—it is not reflective of reality."

It is
NEVER
too LATE
To BE
what you
MIGHT HAVE
~BEEN~

Sleeping beauty

Spraying sheets and pillows with natural sleep oils can be a wonderful aid to slumber

Most people will experience sleep problems at some stage in their life—according to the American Sleep Association, just over 35 percent of adults notch up less than seven hours during a typical 24-hour period. Yet official guidelines suggest that between seven and nine hours are needed for sleep to perform its healing restorative work in adults over the age of 20. So, falling short on Zs on a regular basis isn't great news.

There are many reasons why sleep may give you the runaround. Relationship worries; stress at work; financial concerns—all tend to crowd the mind just when you want to relax, which is why it's worth spending time making the environment you sleep in a tranquil one. Essential oils, which have grown in popularity as an aid to slumber, could help.

Research suggests certain scents, derived from the essential oils of plants, are particularly effective for reducing stress and anxiety and aiding sleep. They can directly impact the body through the nervous system. The olfactory nerve is responsible for the sense of smell and starts from the nose, before entering the skull through tiny holes directly to the brain and sending signals to the limbic system and amygdala, which are linked to emotions, mood, and memory.

These systems are also in charge of regulating the autonomic nervous system, which can either trigger the fight-or-flight response, quickening the breath, heart rate and raising blood pressure, or turn on the parasympathetic nervous system, which relaxes the body. This is part of the reason why scents can trigger physical reactions so quickly, often leaving lasting effects after the scent has gone. The theory is that essential oils react biochemically in much the same way as antianxiety medications do with certain neuroreceptors.

Professor Tim Jacob of Cardiff University in the UK put this theory to the test. His study looked at whether an odor could condition someone to enter the presleep phase and sleep state, inducing the physiological changes associated with rest and relaxation before and during sleep. In laboratory conditions, 23 men and 24 women were exposed to a particular fragrance every night for 28 days. The fragrance was lavender-based, blended with cedarwood, orange, and ylang ylang as other major ingredients.

During this time the participants reported that their quality of sleep improved and researchers recorded a significant reduction in subjects' respiratory rate when exposed to the odor, which became greater as the study continued. Interestingly, the researchers observed that in women there was also a significant impact on blood pressure, although no such effect was evident in men.

The study concluded that a positive feedback loop occurs as the fragrance is repetitively paired with the presleep state. In other words, it's possible to condition the body to relax, ready for sleep, using certain scents.

Turn the page to learn more about fragrances that can help with sleep and to find out which ones might work for you.

Bergamot

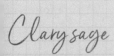

Clary sage

Lavender is well known for its soothing and sedative qualities and is believed to decrease the heart rate and blood pressure

There are a number of ways that essential oils can be used to aid sleep. A few drops can be added to a bath or a soothing, aromatic candle lit before bedtime. They can be diluted with water and diffused into the air or gently rubbed into acupressure points on the body. Pillow mist sprays are increasingly popular as they allow you to sleep in such close proximity to the scent. There are plenty of lovely sprays available to buy or you can make them yourself (see recipe below).

Everyone is different—be prepared for a little trial and error to find the scent that works best when it comes to entering the land of Nod

Lavender
Perhaps the most widely researched fragrance, lavender is well known for its soothing and sedative qualities and is believed to slow down the nervous system and decrease heart rate and blood pressure. A good choice when you want to calm those racing thoughts.

Ylang Ylang
A sweet, floral aromatic extracted from the flower of the cananga tree in Southeast Asia. Light and exotic, it can help to relieve stress and reduce anxiety.

Cedarwood
The deep, woody aroma of cedarwood has been shown to decrease heart rate and blood pressure and has a proven sedative effect.

Jasmine
Pioneered by the ancient Greeks and Egyptians, sweet-smelling jasmine is renowned for its relaxing fragrance. Research on mice suggests it helps soothe, relieve anxiety, and promote rest.

Bergamot
The citrus bergamot is a hybrid fruit, somewhere between a bitter orange and lemon or lime. Recent studies suggest the aroma has the ability to relieve tension and anxiety.

Geranium
This is an uplifting oil with a natural sedative action, thought to be useful in overcoming insomnia. If you have problems getting back to sleep once you've woken in the night, then this could help.

Clary sage
Extracted from the clary sage herb, and a close relative of the common garden herb sage, this essential oil has been used to help people relax during dental procedures and is associated with antidepressant-like effects.

Vetiver
Derived through the steam-distillation of the plant's roots, Vetiver has a strong woody, smoky aroma that is grounding, soothing, and calming, perfect for reducing stress and tension when you're struggling to get to sleep.

HOW TO MAKE
YOUR OWN
PILLOW MIST
SPRAY

Simply add half a cup of water, half a teaspoon of witch hazel, and four to five drops of your favorite essential oil to a spray bottle and shake it up. Gently spray the mist over your pillows before going to bed.

WORDS: GILLIAN ROWE. PHOTOGRAPHS: SHUTTERSTOC.COM

All calm on the home front

Color, texture, light, accessories—all have their part to play in a restful abode. But first you need to work out what's easiest on your eye and your mind. Here's how

Home—somewhere to relax, unwind, and truly be yourself, a calming retreat to return to at the end of a busy day, and a place to escape when you're desperate for time out. Home may vary from person to person—what someone finds cozy and comforting another may find cluttered and chaotic. When it comes to your home, there really are no rules. Your surroundings can play a part in how you feel, however, so it's worth creating an environment that you truly find restful. With a few simple tweaks, it's possible to create an oasis of calm, somewhere you know you can kick back and soothe any woes.

To achieve this serenity, it's good to establish which interiors you find relaxing and to work with what you already have in your home rather than against it. Complementing your existing interior will create a harmonious space and, most of all, it means you won't have to redecorate.

Before you get going, take a little time to think about spaces you find calming. Perhaps you're attracted to traditional country interiors with their charming character and nostalgic feel or maybe you prefer modern, minimalist rooms with an abundance of white space and clean lines. When you have established your preferred style, take a moment to consider how this is achieved. Think about the color scheme, the decorations, the textiles, the lighting, the layout, and even the aromas. Make a note of anything you're particularly drawn to. All of these factors will help you to recreate a similar look and feel in your own home.

Whatever your taste, by highlighting your preference and establishing what it is you find relaxing, you can begin to pinpoint which tones, textures, and ideas you should introduce to give your home the same feelings of calm. And trust me when I say anything is possible—I lived in a tiny rented studio apartment for years and know from experience that you can make even the smallest of spaces feel like a comforting retreat.

Household items

Before you introduce anything new into a room, take a look at what's already in there. If space is limited or you prefer a slightly more minimalist look, you may wish to declutter. Removing anything that no longer serves you—or has a definite purpose—can make a huge difference to the space, especially if you are someone who finds it hard to relax in a busy or cluttered environment.

Color

If you have spent a moment considering what relaxes you, then you should have an idea of your preferred colors. Maybe you're drawn to the cool blues and turquoises of the sea or the warm greens of a forest. Whatever your choice, introducing a few calming shades should change how the room looks and feels. If you don't fancy getting out your paintbrush or you live in rented accommodation where redecorating is not permitted, you could introduce accessories instead, such as cushions, throws, or rugs. This will inject your favorite color with minimal work.

Texture

Adding texture is a great way to make a room feel calm and cozy because it looks and feels comforting and can soften a room. Consider fake fur, fleece, wool, and linen and look out for cushions, blankets, throws, and rugs. In this way, you'll be able to change things around to reflect the seasons, too. Sumptuous throws and soft blankets are perfect for the chilly winter months—add a hot drink and a good book and you'll soon begin to feel at ease.

Lighting

Light and shade can transform the look and feel of a room and it is certainly something to address when creating a calm space. Take a look at the brightness and color of your lamps and, if you have lampshades, look at how they soften and direct the light. Freestanding lamps and sidelights are a great way to tone down the light and add atmosphere. Many can be positioned to give you complete control over where light is projected and help to create a softer and more relaxing mood.

Greenery

Whether you like large palms or cute cacti, there's no denying that houseplants can bring life to a room. By introducing some greenery you can begin to create a natural and serene environment with echoes of the great outdoors. It is lovely to display plants with different patterns, colors, and textures to re-create the calming essence of nature. It's also great to return home to some greenery during the winter months when many trees are bare and flowers are thin on the ground. Houseplants are relatively inexpensive and make lovable housemates too!

Aroma

Naturally scented candles, reed diffusers, essential oils, joss sticks, and pomanders can be used to introduce a welcoming aroma to a space. Choose fragrances that you love and ones that promote relaxation. Unwinding with a magazine, some soothing tunes, and the scent of lavender is a great way to ease the pressures of the day.

Displays

There is something so comforting about being surrounded by your favorite belongings and sentimental items and nothing says "home sweet home" more than the things that bring you joy. Think about new ways you could display photographs and treasured possessions. Be bold and confident with your choices—beautifully illustrated record covers, floral tea cups, or even a gorgeous purse. There's nothing stopping you from enjoying the things that make you smile. Whether you are drawn to 1970s glass or vintage toys, release them from the cupboards to bring a little joy to your everyday.

Turn back the clock...

...and spend an evening at home in 1998

It's raining outside. Come into the house, close the door and kick off your shoes. You have a precious evening at home, with no kids to take care of, no roommates or partners to negotiate. This is your time, to spend as you wish. What are your plans for the night? How will you use these precious few hours between the busyness of daytime and the blank slate of sleep?

Perhaps your ideal evening includes a leisurely meal, and then an hour or so absorbed in a new book. Maybe there's a long soak in a candle-lit bath, followed by a slow settling into bed. Yet best-laid plans don't always work out. You forgot the ingredients for a meal, so have to grab a pizza and salad bag on the way home. Once through the door, your phone pings with an email awaiting a response. You thumb out a reply as the pizza's cooking, and then trawl through the rest of your inbox until the timer beeps.

As you shovel food in your mouth, you keep your mind occupied by checking social media. After dinner, you pick up that book you've been meaning to read. It's hard to concentrate. Your head is still full of memes and rants, you switch on the TV, searching for something that's not too bad. The phone beeps another message, and you tap out a reply while flicking channels.

You need to check likes for your last post, so you're back again on social media, and then try—and fail—to refocus on the TV. You access your movie streaming service, but there are so many to choose from that it's hard to make the right decision. You end up reading reviews online, dismissing your initial choice—and then it's suddenly too late, the TV is on, your phone is pinging, and your eyes are gritty and tired. You stagger to bed and lie in the dark,

wondering why you can't seem to relax, and why your evening wasn't the haven of tranquillity you had hoped for.

Perhaps your realities aren't as extreme as this, but evenings spent at home are not always nurturing. Today people are overwhelmed with choice and addicted to instant gratification. It's not a good combination to enable anyone to switch off in the one place you're supposed to.

There's an ideal to aspire to, though, to create a calm home. It involves healing scents and neutral palettes, Ayurvedic spices, and mindful meditation. As appealing as all that sounds, it can be too huge a leap. A wired-up, overwhelmed brain needs more than turmeric tea.

So, here's a plan to help you relax in the evening and sleep well, without feeling a failure because you've only listened to that mindfulness podcast once this month. You're going to spend an evening 20 years in the past, in 1998 (see our panel, right, for a few pointers). The 1990s was the last decade before the explosion of the digital revolution. Since then, the desire for instant gratification has been granted with ever greater rapidity. In addition, the past 10 years have seen a phenomenal rise in social media usage. Only now is there acknowledgment of its downsides, including its impediment to well-being.

An evening at home in 1998 is the perfect template to navigate a way through the digital minefield. For a start, it's achievable. Evenings at home in the 1990s involved TV and takeout pizza. There was no need to wait for the wireless to warm up or someone to play the piano for entertainment. It was a leisure time you would still recognize today, but without that one crucial factor: overwhelming digital choice.

Try the following when you're granted an evening at home to spend as you wish. Close the door, take off your shoes, and remember that you don't need to have painted your walls taupe to create a sanctuary at home. You just need to pretend it's 1998.

Make your cell phone a landline
Remember owning a landline phone? Turn up your cell's ring and put it in another room, somewhere you won't be tempted to go. Okay, so some of you may have owned cell phones in 1998, but they were used meanly and sparingly. Also, if you do answer the phone, stand well back so you can neither hear properly nor be heard, thus giving you the authentic cell phone experience of the 1990s.

Play music while making dinner
When cooking a meal (or heating a pizza), play an album instead of relying on Spotify. Start listening to the first track and listen all the way through.

Buy a paper TV guide
Get a copy of a TV listings guide, then fetch a pen and circle what you'd like to watch. Anticipate. If you've recorded a show, decide in advance what you'll watch tonight, just like you had to when you only possessed a few bulky video cassettes.

Treat your laptop like an old-fashioned TV
If you don't own a TV, and watch shows on devices, switch off your notifications and put your laptop or tablet out of arm's reach, so you have to cross the room to adjust anything. Do the same with a remote control—the delay before you can access that compulsion to switch might mean you're better able to control it.

Watch a show from start to finish
If halfway through you realize you don't like it, turn it off and read a book instead. Remember, there's nothing on the other channels. And if you're tempted to look up anything, too bad, unless you have an encyclopedia to hand.

And to immerse yourself fully in 1998:
Listen to *I Don't Want to Miss a Thing* by Aerosmith
Watch *Friends*: the one with Ross's wedding
Read *Harry Potter And The Chamber of Secrets* by J.K. Rowling

TURN UP THE MUSIC

Giving your full attention to a piece of music is such a simple way to relax and escape, but when was the last time you slowed down enough to really listen?

When was the last time you listened to music? Not just heard some music, but actually sat down and listened to it. When you think about it, it's not something people do as often as they'd probably like to think.

Everywhere you go these days you're bombarded with music—in bars, restaurants, shopping malls, and grocery stores. You might choose to put some songs on when you're reading, cooking, doing the laundry, driving, eating, or entertaining. Some people even have music on when working. But almost all the time, it's only there as background, a distraction from giving your all to the thing you're doing, while the thing you're doing detracts from appreciating the music.

Being mindful when listening can reintroduce you to the idea of music as a form of relaxation in itself rather than an adjunct to some other activity. It can also help you to fully appreciate the power, beauty, and intricacy of the melody, beat, or voice... because for once you're actually really hearing it.

To do so requires you to fully engage with listening as an experience in its own right. Luckily, there are a few steps to achieving just that. Here's how...

1 Allocate time
Rather than tolerate a love of music as a bolt-on to whatever else seems more important, find some downtime that you're going to devote to listening to music—and do nothing else—even if it's just for 10 or 20 minutes. Choose a time when you can be sure you're not going to be interrupted by family members coming in and out or when you're expecting deliveries or callers.

2 Eradicate distractions
Put the dog in the other room, take the phone off the hook, turn off your cell phone just as you would if you were going to do mindful meditation. Headphones can help keep unwanted auditory distractions out of earshot. Do it at home or in a calm, dedicated space rather than, say, public transport, where you're going to have to make a mental flip to stop thinking about the movements of the people around you or when your stop's coming up.

3 Make yourself comfortable
It really is up to you how. But make sure you're settled, refreshed, and not too hot or too cold before you start, so you don't have to get up to find more cushions, a glass of water, a snack, a sweater—or anything else that could disrupt your engagement with the music. Sit if you like, lie down if you prefer, but make sure you're not going to fall asleep because maintaining a degree of alertness will help you properly engage with the music while remaining relaxed.

4 Choose your medium
Turning off tech is a good move to avoid distractions but it can be impractical when so many people choose to consume music through live streaming services. If you do use them, try to remember to turn off other applications such as email, alerts, and notifications, so that it's just you and the music.

Set up a playlist so you don't have to get ahead of yourself by thinking about the next choice of track—this can stop you really listening. Make sure the playlist is long enough for your intended listening session.

Old-school media such as CDs or vinyl (even cassette) provide a sequence of songs but run the risk of skipping or sticking, requiring attention. Some consider the bumps and clicks on vinyl a feature of their listening pleasure, an extra element to pick out, rather than a fault. The downside? You've only got about 20 minutes before you have to get up and turn over the record.

Choose your music

If you decide on something you know and love, try to overcome the possibility of overfamiliarity by hearing something new that you've never noticed before (see panel, far right, to help you with this exercise). It can be easier to be more curious about a track when it's less familiar, so this could be the time to engage with that new album someone's been raving about. And remember, this is about enjoying music, any music, from rap to Rachmaninov and death metal to Debussy. There's no pressure to unearth the slowed-down beats of relaxation songs.

Take a mindful approach

Treat it in much the same way as you would any other activity you might approach in a mindful way—walking, for example. This might involve two minutes of really looking at the things around you, followed by two of really listening to the sounds you hear, a couple focusing on smells, and two on sensations to do with touch, such as the feel of the wind, sun, or rain on the face.

Of course, with music you're only really interested in the listening part, so first of all close your eyes. Then take a similar approach to the walking scenario, here focusing on the different components that make a contribution to the whole sound. For most tracks, two minutes on each will be too long, so you could concentrate instead for 30 seconds on the guitar, then the vocal, then the bass, then the drums and then other elements. Finally, take time to relax your focus to take in the song as a whole.

Enjoy it

Just as with mindful meditation the idea is to be curious, from second to second and bar to bar, just as you're curious about each in-breath and out-breath. Gently note what you hear: Is the music soft or hard, does it build or dip or is it repetitive, is it dense or minimalist, quiet or loud, luxurious or Spartan, dextrous or simple? Remember that it's also supposed to be about relaxation and enjoyment, not an exam, so the focus should be light, soft, and effortless—don't be hard on yourself if your mind drifts. When it does, bring your focus back to the music, just as you would to the breath when meditating. Likewise, if the music stirs certain emotions, note them and return your attention to what you're hearing in the moment.

The live music experience

Gigs and festivals are more important ways of consuming music than they've ever been. But they're also an arena where it's easy to be distracted by what someone's wearing, the movements of the band, or the lights. They're all important in helping make the occasion what it is, but dialing them down for a few minutes can enhance your experience of the music. Closing your eyes helps. You can then follow the mindful listening routine already described or sink into the music's texture, richness, subtlety, grittiness, pain, virtuosity, or lyrical prowess. If listening to the music stirs your emotions or thoughts, you can include those inner experiences as an extension of the music and appreciation practice.

LISTEN AFRESH TO...

Lou Reed: Walk On The Wild Side

Everyone knows this; it's the one with the backing vocals that go "Do, do-do, do, do-do-do-do." It's a great track for an exercise in mindful listening because it builds gradually with different instrumental elements dropping in and out.

0.00	It starts with a single note, followed by a succession of pairs of notes, on an upright acoustic bass, with a gently strumming acoustic guitar behind.
0.11	The drums come in, but played softly with brushes rather than sticks, helping to create a gentle lilting sound.
0.20	Reed's lead vocal comes in: resonant but vulnerable... and crystal clear, allowing you to engage with the story of the song, not just its sound.
0.38	A second bass line, played on an electric bass comes in, adding a slightly mournful note, drops out at 0.58 before coming back at 1.10.
1.25	In response to Reed's lead, those famous female backing vocals make their first appearance, just for 15 seconds or so.
1.45	A gentle, sweeping violin line drifts in, taking its cue from the vocal melody and developing into an instrumental flourish between verses. It goes on like this a while until...
2.35	The acoustic bass suddenly jumps to a four-note pattern, just for a few bars, and Lou makes a little yelp between verses.
3.10	Lou goes full on "Do, do-do, do, do-do-do-do" and the backing singers pick up the refrain. All this time you can still pick out the two bass lines, the brushed drums and the guitar rhythm. Then...
3.37	The vocals drop and a single soft brushed cymbal heralds a baritone sax solo that meanders into the distance as the song fades.
4.10	The end.

NOTES

Note to self

You may have kept a journal as a teenager, diligently writing your private thoughts, treasured hopes, and every detail of adolescent angst. So why not return to a notebook today?

One of the things often left behind in the transition from teenager to adulthood is the habit of keeping a journal. Yet taking the time to write as an adult can lead to invaluable insight. In the quiet moments of reflection that writing can offer, feelings and concerns can be explored, as can creative ideas. The future can become clear, as can the past. As words appear on the page, it's possible to move from the imaginary into the present, to understand and write new histories, to gain a healing perspective by investing in storytelling that's deeply personal.

"Our notebooks give us away, for however dutifully we record what we see around us, the common denominator of all we see is always, transparently, shamelessly, the implacable 'I,'" writes essayist Joan Didion in her essay, On Keeping a Notebook, in *Slouching Towards Bethlehem*. Likening her habit to a compulsion, Joan views the need to write as an entirely personal one. A disposition born not from the desire accurately to record everyday events, but from a personality type that views the world through the lens of a relentless why. Returning to the subject again in her 1976 essay Why I Write, she adds: "I write entirely to find out what I'm thinking, what I'm looking at, what I see, and what it means. What I want and what I fear."

Regardless of the motivation, keeping a notebook is deeply personal. Writing on a regular basis is to have an ongoing conversation with the self, which takes place between the world as experienced and an interpretation of it. Absorbed in the free flow of thoughts and ideas, events and relationships can suddenly be seen in a new light. The future can be imagined with steps of how to get there. There can be moments of insight that even

surprise, as if through the very act of putting pen to paper, they are given life for the first time.

Keeping a notebook is therefore a way to discover and even reconnect with different selves. An afternoon spent reading through old notebooks can reignite passions, lead to a revival of interests, and a new sense of commitment. "In the journal I do not just express myself more openly than I could do to any person; I create myself," wrote academic and author, Susan Sontag. "The journal is a vehicle for my sense of selfhood."

Such is the power of this self-narrative that journal writing can help with mindfulness, focus thoughts, shape how events and memories are viewed, and even promote a more positive outlook. It has also been used as a tool in therapy as a way of working through traumatic events.

In their study, Counting Blessings Versus Burdens, where they investigated gratitude and well-being in daily life, psychologists Robert A. Emmons and Michael E. McCullough asked participants to record their moods, behaviors, and physical symptoms related to a series of assigned topics. The group that wrote what they were grateful for reported at the end of the study that they felt more optimistic, had increased their levels of physical exercise, and experienced fewer health problems.

Similarly, Joshua M. Smyth et al studied the impact of writing on the physical symptoms of asthma and rheumatoid arthritis patients. Participants were asked to write for 20 minutes on three consecutive days a week. Those assigned to write about the most stressful event of their lives demonstrated clinical improvements four months after the writing exercise: "Writing helped patients get better, and also kept them from getting worse."

> *"But what is more to the point is my belief that the habit of writing thus for my own eye only is good practice. It loosens the ligaments. Never mind the misses and the stumbles"*
>
> VIRGINIA WOOLF

Such is the power of words that they can help with goal achievement. According to Gail Matthews, a psychology professor at the Dominican University in California, people are 42 percent more likely to achieve their goals when they write them down on a regular basis.

Writing and creativity

Unlike a diary, where events are chronicled, a notebook can foster creativity, experimentation, and freedom of ideas. The celebrated notebooks of artists and writers such as Anaïs Nin and Virginia Woolf attest to this. Episodic, frequently unstructured, ranging from detailed vignettes of daily life to half-formed dialogues and conversations, such writings show the imagination at play and the importance of this playfulness to the creative process. Speaking of keeping a diary, Anaïs shared that in writing she discovered "improvisation, free association, obedience to mood, impulse, brought forth countless images, portraits, descriptions, impressionistic sketches, symphonic experiments, from which I could dip at any time for material." Published during her lifetime, 16 diaries explore the subjects of love and passion, the meaning of life and the essence of creativity, and are as important as her novels and short stories for understanding her literary oeuvre.

Similarly, Virginia Woolf spoke of the creative benefits of keeping a diary. She viewed the practice as key to the process of writing—"It loosens the ligaments. Never mind the misses and the stumbles"—and as fundamental to creativity. In a diary entry from April 20 1919, she shared:

"I should like to come back, after a year or two, and find that the collection had sorted itself and refined itself and coalesced, as such deposits so mysteriously do, into a mold, transparent enough to reflect the light of our life, and yet steady, tranquil compounds with the aloofness of a work of art."

In other words, ideas can initially appear as fleeting or transient. It is only over time that they can congeal and take tangible form. Journal writing captures this process but also aids it.

Beyond the written word

The written word is extraordinarily compelling, but creativity can also take flight through the world of color, texture, and shape. A collage, moodboard, or even the random assemblage of found objects—a train ticket, a photo torn from a magazine, a sample of cloth—all of these are talismen for different journeys and self-expression.

Mexican artist Frida Kahlo kept notebooks exploring the themes of death and illness, Mexican art and culture, self-portraiture, and surrealism for the 10 years leading up to her death. Published posthumously, they are filled with intensely colored watercolors and thoughts, dreams, and poems. Deeply personal and emotively raw, the contents reveal Frida's creative process and are an intimate portrait of herself, arguably more moving than her self-portraits.

Notebooks can take numerous forms. Use one to note down daily observations and ideas that interest you. A "life book" could be filled with collages, occasionally annotated with reflections and aspirations. Between the pages you could keep treasured letters and postcards that you've received, alongside photos of loved ones. Think of each page as an imaginary landscape that you have created from the world around you. There doesn't need to be any logic to when you choose to add to it. Do remember though, your notebook isn't somewhere to store stories you're telling others, just ones for yourself.

TAKING YOUR FIRST STEPS IN KEEPING A NOTEBOOK

Fill your pages daily In her book *The Artist's Way*, author Julia Cameron explores the connection between creativity and writing. Likening creativity to a muscle that must be worked, she encourages people to write three pages a day and to write without thinking. Such streams of consciousness allow for thoughts and ideas to arise and to unlock what she believes to be people's innate creativity.

Express gratitude By writing a sentence a day, Gretchen Rubin, who's responsible for a weekly Happier podcast, states that people can keep "happy memories vivid." Realistic and highly pragmatic, her approach encourages an ongoing chronicle of personal quests for happiness and what has been achieved.

Explore the power of the visual Collect photos, pictures from magazines, postcards, and even dried flowers, ribbons, and leaves to create a working collection of images. Intuitively bring colors and textures together before trying to capture in words what they represent to you.

Mind over matter

Be inspired to live in the moment with these mindful words

Be happy in the moment, that's enough. Each moment is all we need, not more.

Mother Teresa

Training your mind to be in the present moment is the number one key to making healthier choices.

Susan Albers

In today's rush, we all think too much, seek too much, want too much, and forget about the joy of just being.

Eckhart Tolle

Nothing can dim the light that shines from within.

Maya Angelou

Our own worst enemy cannot harm us as much as our unwise thoughts. No one can help us as much as our own compassionate thoughts.

Buddha

Look for the answer inside your question.

Rumi

Pure awareness transcends thinking. It allows you to step outside the chattering negative self-talk and your reactive impulses and emotions. It allows you to look at the world once again with open eyes. And when you do so, a sense of wonder and quiet contentment begins to reappear in your life.

Mark Williams

The mind is like water. When it's turbulent, it's difficult to see. When it's calm, everything becomes clear.

Prasad Mahes

Happiness is your nature. It is not wrong to desire it. What is wrong is seeking it outside when it is inside.

Ramana Maharshi

Life is a dance. Mindfulness is witnessing that dance.

Amit Ray

The little things? The little moments? They aren't little.

Jon Kabat-Zinn

Mind is a flexible mirror, adjust it, to see a better world.

Amit Ray, *Mindfulness Living In The Moment*—Living In The Breath

Mindfulness is like that—it is the miracle which can call back in a flash our dispersed mind and restore it to wholeness so that we can live each minute of life.

Thich Nhat Hanh, *The Miracle Of Mindfulness: An Introduction To The Practice Of Meditation*

Your calm mind is the ultimate weapon against your challenges. So relax.

Bryant McGill, *Simple Reminders: Inspiration For Living Your Best Life*

Mindfulness is simply being aware of what is happening right now without wishing it were different; enjoying the pleasant without holding on when it changes (which it will); being with the unpleasant without fearing it will always be this way (which it won't).

James Baraz

Made in the USA
Monee, IL
29 April 2022

95611360R00059